SHOES OF PEACE
Letters to Youth from Peacemakers

Brethren Press·

~

~

Contents

Introduction — Julie Garber

Epitaph

Introduction

You may wonder what the generations that brought you the bloodiest century since the birth of Christ have to say to you about peace. Perhaps it would have been better for adults to sit back for once and listen to the fresh perspectives of youth. Perhaps you will do better than we did, so far as it depends on you, to live peaceably with all (Rom.12:18).

But these letters were not written as an example for you to follow. They don't have great successes to share. They don't represent a growing movement. In fact, the writers are part of a minuscule minority for peace in a world that mainly operates by force. Instead, these letters to you are an accounting of the hope that is within us (1 Pet. 3:15).

The people whose letters you will read in this book have stepped over the lines of authority, facing right up to life-threatening danger. Some have been sent to prison and hauled into court; some have withheld a little of themselves from violent governments by not paying war taxes or by declaring themselves conscientious objectors on their Selective Service forms. All of them have stayed true to the teachings of Christ as far as they were able. They did it not because they take pride in suffering or because suffering will earn them a place in heaven. They are witnesses for peace because there is joy in it. It's not perfection they seek, but the deep satisfaction and fulfillment that comes with putting faith into action.

Sound a little scary and a little dangerous? One of the most often repeated instructions in the New Testament is "do not be afraid." Fear—fear of the enemy, fear of violence, fear of judgment, fear of governments, fear of poverty, fear of rejection, fear of uncertainty—is a trap. Whatever we fear is very likely to happen to us, because these things will happen in life anyway. Fear will not make death go away. But joy and faith can make death less important. Fear of the enemy will not do anything to save us from an opponent, but love and joy can change an enemy to a friend. Fear won't end world poverty, but biblical justice can. At the end of the day, it will be more scary if we give in to fear and abandon Jesus' way of peace.

These letters are a testimony for you that real joy in life comes from bold and active faith. Live the gospel and you will find the greatest success—that the kingdom of joy and light is at hand. With Ted Studebaker every peacemaker can say "Life is great, yea!"

Julie Garber
2002

P.S. The mail keeps coming in. To see more letters on peace, visit **www.shoesofpeace.org.** Or submit your own letter for possible posting on the website. Go to the website for instructions.

LETTER ONE
Sarah Leatherman Young

Dear youth,

First of all, let me remind you that you are the joy of our hearts and our hope for the future. It is not only your parents who love you—you have many spiritual aunties, uncles, and grandparents rooting for you from the pews of your church. All those Sunday school teachers, camp counselors, choir directors, and pastors who have cared for you in some little way through the years rejoice and thank God for you as they see you grow toward adulthood and mature in the Lord. I pray that we have equipped you well for life's journey; that is, in part, the purpose of this book and this letter.

Bette Midler once said, "Give a girl the correct footwear and she can conquer the world!" That's probably a bit much; after all, you wouldn't want to be obsessed with shoes. I just really like shoes. Colorful shoes. In part, it comes from my artistic nature (when I was your age I was really into fashion illustration). In part, it comes out of reaction to the years of elementary school when I was stuck in maroon Buster Brown oxfords, because I had a foot problem and couldn't wear all the cute shoes that my classmates did. But shoes are something we all need, and we need different types to fit different situations: work shoes, dress shoes, boots for winter, and sandals for summer.

I know this all sounds very frivolous, but I *do* have a point. You see, I've discovered that some of my favorite scripture verses about *peace* also have to do with *feet*! For example, Isaiah 52:7: "How beautiful upon the mountains are the feet of the messenger who announces peace." The solo in Handel's *The Messiah* says it even more poetically: "How beautiful are the feet of those who preach the gospel of peace!"

The verse I want to lift up to you in this letter, however, is Ephesians 6:15: "*As shoes for your feet put on whatever will make you ready to proclaim the gospel of peace*." This verse is from the "whole armor of God" passage, which some Brethren don't like to use because of the military image. But friends, this passage is talking about spiritual warfare in the world, which is a reality. So we had better be well equipped. And as a member of a pacifist church, I want to pay special attention to the gear on my feet. What is it that will make me ready to proclaim the gospel of peace?

I like to play with the symbolism in this verse and envision the footwear of those who were great at proclaiming peace. I think of the simple shoes of Mother Teresa covered with the dust of Calcutta, the bishops' shoes of Desmond Tutu as he held hearings to reconcile the evils of apartheid. I think of the work shoes of peacemaking men of the soil from our own tradition like Ted Studebaker and Dan West.

I see in my mind's eye Dr. Martin Luther King, Jr., in a pair of big, glorious, white marching boots. Why? Because when people tried to put him down as a "drum major" as he led people in nonviolent action against racism, he turned their own words on them and said, "Yes, if you want to say that I was a drum major, say that I was a drum major for justice. Say that I was a drum major for peace. Say that I was a drum major for righteousness. And all of the other shallow things will not matter."

I think about peacemakers like Gandhi and St. Francis, who took off the shoes of privilege to walk barefoot in solidarity with the poor.

The feet of all I mention were shod differently, yet their feet were equipped to preach peace in their own unique way, in their own setting.

I encourage you to expand the metaphor for yourself. How will you equip *your* feet to preach the gospel of peace? Start thinking about it now, because this is the kind of thing you need to plan in advance—like buying winter boots before there's a foot of snow on the ground!

Secondly, I can't choose for you what skills will best equip you, anymore than I can choose your shoes. You may have to try on many different things before you find just the right style and fit for you. But I *can* recommend some of the things that have worn the best for me over time.

1. *Get to know as many different types of people as possible.* The more we know and respect people of different cultures, races, religions, and classes, the more absurd it is to think of them as "the enemy." Visit them where they live, whether that's across the globe or across town.

2. *Know alternatives to violence.* Become trained in mediation. Advocate for justice. Study the words and works of Jesus and famous peacemakers.

3. *Find inner peace.* When we're mad at ourselves inside, we're more apt to lash out at others. It's important to be gentle and loving with ourselves.

4. *Pray for the gift of peacemaking.* Try reciting "Make Me an Instrument of Your Peace" everyday.

My prayers and blessings are with you as you search for the right fit. Who knows? Maybe with the right footwear you *can* conquer the world. Conquer it with the peace of Christ.

In peace,
Sarah Leatherman Young

Sarah Leatherman Young is pastor of Prince of Peace Church of the Brethren in Littleton, Colorado.

LETTER TWO
David Radcliff

Dear friends,

"To kill or *not* to kill" is not the only question. Of course, I hope that if it ever comes right down to it and you have to make a decision about going to war, you'll just say no. And I hope you'll base this on Jesus' words about loving our enemies, on Church of the Brethren teachings that all war is sin, and on your own deep respect for human life. These were some of the things that motivated me to be a conscientious objector during the Vietnam War.

If you're lucky, you won't be faced with the question of personally going to war. But that doesn't mean you're off the hook. Jesus didn't say, "Blessed are the noncombatants." He said, "Blessed are the peacemakers." What does it mean to be a peacemaker in a world like ours?

For one thing, violence doesn't just happen on the battlefield. The number one cause of injury to young women in our society is violence inflicted by a dating partner or other male acquaintance. Every month, 25 percent of kids miss a day of school for fear of being bullied. People of color in this country get less respect than others when they're in the court system, in the doctor's office, and in everyday life—and that's a kind of institutional violence.

Look around our world. With 25 percent of all the world's people living on less than $1 a day, injustice is sowing the seeds of violence. Religious and ethnic differences make people suspicious of each other—or cause them to do worse things. And the nations, with ours leading the pack, spend 100 times more on the military than on reaching out to the world's poor.

You can see that choosing to be a peacemaker can take you in lots of directions. But don't worry, you won't be going there alone—or even first. Jesus has been there before, and walks with you now. Brethren women and men have gone ahead, breaking the trail and showing us how it's done.

Of course, not everybody takes this path—but nonconformity is something people like you aren't afraid of. So what will you do with yourself and your life to make the world a more peaceful and secure place for people everywhere? *That* really is the question.

Peace to you—and to our world,
David Radcliff

David Radcliff is director of Brethren Witness, Church of the Brethren General Board.

LETTER THREE
David R. Miller

Dear Brethren youth,

Jesus is the way. He only wrecked the temple once, and I think John has it right to put it so early in the Gospel (John 2). We know right off the bat that things are going to be different with him. The way we normally think about religion and faith and being a good person is nice, but it's dead. That's precisely what Jesus is judging when he turns over the tables in the temple and drives out the money changers. Jesus wants us to really live, so he runs us out of the temple, which is a symbol of convention and the status quo.

And even as Jesus was furiously driving people out of the temple, he was giving them a chance to see differently—he wasn't killing them. He was begging them to drink the new and better wine. He didn't trust people who were impressed that he could do signs. That's why he's not impressed by Nicodemus (John 3:1-3). Nicodemus talks about the signs Jesus does: "Wow! Your power must be from God." But the power Jesus is talking about and is releasing into the world can't be seen with MTV eyes or Oxford eyes for that matter. That's why we must be transformed.

We have to forget asking, "What if I am hurt? What if others are hurt? Isn't it natural to fight?" These are all fine questions, but they are not Jesus' questions. His first desire is for us to be changed as from ordinary water into good wine. That's the only way Christ's peace comes into the world—when we forget the temples, when we are not impressed by, or afraid of, power and money and looks and muscles and death and life. "Do you want to be made well?" (John 5:6) Do you want Christ's peace? Do you? Do we? Then stand up and walk!

In Christ's name,
David R. Miller

David R. Miller is pastor of First Church of the Brethren in Roanoke, Virginia, and a non-registrant for the draft.

LETTER FOUR
Ted Studebaker

TED STUDEBAKER
DI LINH VILLAGE
VIETNAM

My home in Di Linh

Ted Studebaker went to Vietnam not as a soldier, but as a BVS volunteer working for Vietnam Christian Service as an agriculturalist. His job was to help local farmers, among other things, increase their crop yield and improve their flocks of chicken. The people with whom he worked, the Montagnards, were suspected by the rebel Vietcong of being collaborators with the South Vietnamese government, and on April 25, 1971, the Vietcong raided the village where he lived and killed Ted. That night before the raid he had finished writing a letter to a family at home in the United States that was critical of his peace position. Here are some excerpts from his response.

I do not "feel the enemy is right" any more than I feel the US military is "right" here.... I believe strongly in trying to follow the example of Jesus Christ as best I know how. Above all, Christ taught me to love all people, including enemies, and to return good for evil, and that all men are brothers in Christ. I condemn all war and consciously refuse to take part in it in any active or violent way. I believe love is a stronger and more enduring power than hatred for my fellow men, regardless of who they are or what they believe.

...You probably think I'm pretty idealistic and, by your letter, indicate that I'm a pretty mixed up kid. But, I cannot apologize for any part of the letter I wrote to my church, since it well represents honestly and sincerely my feelings and concerns about this particular situation. I have tried to speak from both experience and reason, not from mere emotion or hearsay"

... Please know that I am in excellent health and adequate safety. I know I am a fortunate man and life is great to me....

Life is great, yea.

Reprinted from Messenger *(15 June 1971). Used by permission.*

LETTER FIVE
Barbara Sayler

Dear sisters,

If you know me, you know that much of the time my thinking runs counter to what much of our society is thinking—or so it seems. I tend to fight the system and ask questions that people don't always want to answer or even think about. I try to think outside the box about how the excluded can be included, the voiceless can be heard, the marginalized can find their place at the table. Do you ever feel any of these things?

There are times when I get overwhelmed with all of this and just want to escape into the mainstream, just to think and be like everyone else. Wouldn't my life be so much easier? Wouldn't I be happier and feel more accepted, if I supported the military action that is happening in so many parts of our world, or if I joined the corporate world doing work that expands the economy, but does little for the good of humankind; or if I sat silently in worship and church meetings? Wouldn't I? But how would I feel when I heard the daily news about the lives of people in Afghanistan or Palestine? And how would I feel when I passed a homeless person on the street? How would I feel when I sat in a church council meeting and my brother is not heard because he is gay or my sister is ignored because she is female? And how would I feel when I read Micah's words "to do justice, and to love kindness, and to walk humbly with [our] God"—and Jesus' words to love both our neighbors and our enemies, and to go the second mile, and to watch out for the specks in our own eyes? How do some of these things make you feel?

How would I feel? For me, this question has a major impact on the decisions I continually make in my life. I might be able to convince myself that I could be happier, more accepted, and more like everyone else if I changed my thinking; but my feelings would eventually take over again, because these concerns for others are more than a fleeting emotion and come from my inner being, from what I believe, from the very basis of my faith in God. They come from my experiences in Brethren Volunteer Service, in the relationships that I build with brothers and sisters, and in being a woman in ministry.

My passion for peace began when people finally listened to me and I discovered that I had been silenced for years without realizing it. This passion increased as I was heard and as I also heard from others those things I had not allowed myself to absorb before. I felt like a sponge, just soaking it all up. I began to imagine the possibility of how the world might be if we allowed the things that make for peace to enter into our being and doing. I wondered how our society (not to mention our church) might change if we were to follow Paul's words in Romans 12 that call us to transform our relationships and increase our intimate circle. Might this be enough to overcome evil with good? With this wonder and possibility, I have not only changed, but I am hopeful that peace can happen and that the violent norms of our society today don't have to be the norms of the future.

Do you wonder any of these things? What are the possibilities you imagine for the world or for the church? Do you believe that through peace, through faith and love we can change the world?

I hope you will ask even the hard questions—and not get too hung up on finding all the answers. My dream for you is that you will seek opportunities and relationships that will nurture your faith and your being as you imagine the possibilities for peace.

Shalom,
Barb Sayler

Barbara Sayler is co-executive director of On Earth Peace Assembly.

LETTER SIX
Bob Gross

Dear sisters and brothers,

Let me start out with a warning: you have to watch out for Sunday school. It can be a very radicalizing experience. All those lessons about "God loves everyone" and "love your enemies" can shape a young child early. The child may never recover. I know I didn't. I just kept on believing those things they taught me, and it got me into all kinds of trouble later on.

Today, when a young man turns eighteen, he is expected to register for the draft. If he chooses to do so, he just fills out a form at the post office and that's pretty much the end of it. In 1968, when I reached that magic age, things were a little different. After registering at age eighteen, every man was issued a "draft card," which indicated his status with the draft. He was supposed to carry that card at all times. And the big difference was that a lot of young men were being drafted into the military, because the United States was fighting a war in Vietnam.

When I registered for the draft, I signed up as a conscientious objector. I still believed what my Sunday school teachers had taught me, and I knew that I could not kill anyone. As a conscientious objector, I could still be drafted, but I would be sent to do some kind of civilian work (called alternative service) instead of military service.

A year and a half later, I joined Brethren Volunteer Service (BVS), which was one way of doing my alternative service. I was sent to inner-city Baltimore for my first project; the draft people approved it, so we were all set.

Well, not for long.

Even though I liked and believed in what I was doing on my BVS project, I felt really bad about carrying a draft card. It seemed like I was carrying a membership card in the whole war system. And although my card said that I could do civilian work instead of military duty, I knew there were a lot of other young men whose cards said they had to go to Vietnam. So after a lot of prayer and a lot of talking to people about it, I decided to return my draft card and began a new project doing peace education. I was able to complete my second year of BVS before being indicted for resisting the draft.

When I went to court, I persuaded the judge to let me represent myself instead of having a lawyer speak for me. I decided not to put on a legal defense, so I pleaded guilty to the charges. That way we could skip the trial and go right to the sentencing, where I could have people speak in my behalf and we could bear witness to our beliefs. The sentencing hearing went well, and we had a chance to speak up for Jesus' way of peace, but the judge was not moved. I was sentenced to three years in federal prison and served half of that time before being released on parole.

For me, the choice of non-cooperation with the draft was an attempt to be faithful to what I believe God was calling me to do. People often suggested I would be "more effective" if I would compromise with the government and thereby stay out of jail. As it turned out, witnessing in this way probably had more effect on more people than anything else I could have done. I have never regretted choosing that path.

The way I see it, only God can overcome violence, hate, domination, militarism, racism, and all the other evils I would like to do away with, and so the most *effective* thing I can do is to be faithful to what I believe God is calling me to do. Basically, it's just looking for what God is doing in the world and trying to be part of that.

Each war is a time of testing our commitment to our belief in Jesus' way. Each war is an opportunity to witness to that way—to live out the lessons we learned in Sunday school.

Now the United States is at war again, a "war on terrorism," which could go on forever, creating more hatred of the US and more would-be terrorists every day. Paul says it clearly in Romans 12:21: "Do not be overcome by evil, but overcome evil with good." There is no other way to overcome evil—Jesus made that plain in his Sermon on the Mount—but it seems that our national leaders have not gotten the message.

So it's up to us, who *do* get Jesus' message, to pass that good news on to others. The Church of the Brethren is one of the few churches that teaches the gospel of peace as Jesus taught it, and that is both a blessing and a responsibility for you as a youth growing up in this church. I hope you make the most of it. On Earth Peace, Brethren Witness, and other groups in the church will work with you. Through them, you can find information, inspiration, and connections with other youth and adults who share your beliefs and questions.

And one more thing. I hope you push the church to live up to Jesus' call to peacemaking. Expect the church to live up to the things they teach you in Sunday school. That stuff about loving your enemies and overcoming evil with good is the truth. If the church doesn't live that way, who will?

In peace,
Bob Gross

Bob Gross is a professional conflict mediator and co-executive director of On Earth Peace Assembly.

LETTER SEVEN
Andrew Murray

Dear one,

In ordinary times, it is not difficult to be for peace. Peace seems to be the norm. Sometimes we even look back on our bloody history and wonder, somewhat smugly, why people could not learn to live together. In ordinary times, it is easy to let our attention drift to making our lives comfortable, successful, and fun. It is easy to lose sight of the struggles that have produced our comfort and to become complacent about the inequities that may help perpetuate our success and our fun.

When trouble comes, on the other hand, we may be unprepared to meet the destructive energies unleashed by ancient hatreds and contemporary struggles for power. In troubled times, when we feel that our way of life is genuinely threatened, when we may feel unjustly accused and despised, when we feel misunderstood and disrespected, it may be easy to begin to think that the way of peace is the way of weakness.

In troubled times, those who will ask, maybe even demand, that you wear a uniform and carry a weapon will tell you that liberty and peace are not cheap. They will be right. They will tell you that nothing good comes without struggle. They will be right. They will tell you that one must show courage in the face of evil and that one must be willing to stand up for and to defend those who cannot defend themselves. They will be right.

They may also tell you that the only way to do this is to be willing to practice the same violence as those who do evil. They will be wrong. They may tell you that in the *real* world, enemies only understand the language of violence. They will be wrong. They may tell you that history proves that peace can only be guaranteed to those who are ready and willing to be successful at war. They will be wrong. They may tell you that there is only one way to fight. They will be wrong.

Mohandas Gandhi, Henry David Thoreau, Martin Luther King, Jr., Nelson Mandela, and Cesar Chavez were all fighters. Mary Dyer, Sojourner Truth, Susan B. Anthony, Jane Addams, and Emma Goldman were all fighters. In our tradition Dan West, John Kline, M. R. Zigler, Sarah Major, Anna Mow, and Ted Studebaker were all fighters. They did not use weapons to defend their truth. Truth was their weapon. They did not use weapons to show their courage. Courage was their weapon. They were not willing to make others suffer in order to change the world. They were willing to accept the suffering that a changing world inevitably brings.

In fact, times are never quite as ordinary, or as troubled, as they may seem. Those who suffer the injustice of exploitation do not disappear in normal times. They simply become less visible. The struggle continues, but it seems further away. Indeed, when complacency is the norm, it is the time to double one's fight and to double one's preparation. When the passions of fear and revenge seem to be the norm, it is time to double one's serenity and thoughtfulness. When the storm laps at our shore, it is time to use the preparations made in calmer times.

As followers of Christ, we are called to struggle for a different kingdom, a different social order, one that is marked by reconciliation and fairness rather than revenge and privilege; one that is marked by a struggle for truth rather than a struggle for control. It is to the vision of this kingdom that we owe our first allegiance. In both ordinary times and troubled times, people of conscience may choose different courses of action, but we cannot choose to put our allegiance elsewhere. And we cannot choose to skip the struggle.

In Christ,
Andy Murray

Andrew Murray is Elizabeth Evans Baker Professor of Religion and Peace and Conflict Studies and director of the Baker Institute for Peace and Conflict Studies at Juniata College.

LETTER EIGHT
Ken Brown

Nicholas Jones
255 Maple Drive
Cottage, Tennessee 97314

Dear Brethren youth,

If you tell almost anyone that Jesus really meant it when he called us to be peacemakers, the first question you may well hear is, "But what about Hitler?" After all, Hitler started World War II, conquered most of Europe, and killed some eleven million people, including six million Jews in extermination camps. Had he not been stopped, you will be told, we would be speaking German and the moral values of western civilization would have been forever lost. Even if all other wars turned out to be unnecessary, wasn't our fight against Hitler and the Nazis the "Good War," which we absolutely *had* to fight?

Of course, there may be no good answer as to how to save a house already engulfed by flames, or a ship already floundering in a hurricane. No answer seems adequate. Yes, the horrible evils of fascism had to be fought, but buried in the usual reply is the assumption that we had to fight Hitler with the same terrible weapons that the Germans used against us. Our "civilization" has used violence and war so often that we have tunnel vision and don't even try to look for other possible methods.

Try looking outside the tunnel. It's true that war stopped Hitler from enslaving and killing others, but were it not for the way the winners of World War I punished Germany, the loser, you and history would never have heard of Adolph Hitler. *War*, not pacifism, gave us Hitler. True enough, war finally stopped the mass killings in the Nazi death camps, but again, if there had been no *war*, there probably would never have been death camps. The Nazis researched several ways, including forced deportation, to carry out their irrational hatred against Jews and others they considered enemies. Again, *total war,* which aims at killing as many of the enemy as possible in every conceivable way, brought the Nazis to use horrendous death camps to exterminate millions of Jews, homosexuals, gypsies, communists, and others. The Allies ignored the camps and concentrated on winning the war militarily, but brave people in Denmark, Norway, Sweden, and Bulgaria shook off tunnel vision and by creative non-cooperation saved more of their Jewish neighbors than they ever could have rescued with weapons. Nonviolent resistance, rather than guns, worked even against the Nazi war machine.

The other reason given for war against Hitler was to stop his conquest of Eastern Europe, Russia, then England and the world. Again, almost everybody assumes that military resistance was the only possible response to the German war machine that swept through most of Europe and all the way to Stalingrad in Russia. Think outside the box. Could 55 million Germans have controlled 95 million Eastern Europeans and 155 million Russians for long if they had resisted by every possible means of non-cooperation? As Gibbon, the historian who wrote about the fall of Rome, writes, "There is nothing more contrary to nature than to attempt to hold in obedience distant provinces." Yes, there would have been much repression and many deaths, but would the costs have been as high as military victory—cities and economies destroyed, 50 million people killed, and the world subjected to the curse of nuclear weapons and the arms race between the United States and the Soviet Union? Do we overrate the Nazis and ignore the reality that in defeating the German expansion by war, we substituted Stalin for Hitler in Eastern Europe, one repressive dictator for another? Do we count the other costs of fighting fire with fire, bombs with bombs—our entire planet threatened by stockpiles of nuclear weapons, spawned in radioactive cesspools, awaiting accident or the folly of policies like the formation of Mutually Assured Destruction (MAD)?

Does tunnel vision prevent us from seeing the spiritual deformity and moral hideousness in our own threat to destroy entire continents of people and natural resources in our pursuit of wealth and security? World War II gave us nuclear weapons, a curse that we have not yet learned to cure. Our country possesses the largest capability for mass killing, which we jealously guard against others. There can be no real peace so long as *any* country has nuclear weapons.

By fighting Hitler on his own terms, we had to become too much like him. He militarized his society. We militarized. He drafted young men for killing. We drafted young men for killing. He killed millions of innocent people by carting them to the ovens of his death camps. We killed millions of innocent people by carting the ovens to the people, bombing their homes and cities into oblivion. Josef Goebbels, propaganda chief for the Nazis, once said that even if the Germans lost the war, their *spirit* would prevail. If he was right, there is little hope for your generation. Violence brings more violence; vengeance reaps vengeance; and you will be caught up in the dreadful hatreds that spew out death.

There is another possibility, another path out. Hitler had to be fought, but with weapons so different that they wouldn't multiply the evil. Violence is not like a cancer that can be cut out, leaving the rest of the body unharmed. Violence is more like an infection that spreads throughout the body and can be cured only by strong antidotes to the disease. Violence cannot cure violence any more than infection can cure infection. War is a poor way to prepare for peace. The tunnel vision of war does not make for peace. God teaches us to act, to refuse obedience to the evil of the world, and to fight with the weapons of the spirit. Those weapons include protest of evil, non-cooperation, forgiveness, kindness, friendship, charity, and hope.

Will the weapons of the spirit always work? Sometimes nonviolence seems to fail while war can and does drastically change things. But faith in Christ means that we hold fast to the power of love even when we cannot possibly see the consequences. Our faith in love gives us hope.

What about Hitler? He was the product of war and the cause of more war. Whatever we decide about that past, it is certain that our future cannot survive the horrible disease of modern warfare. In every daily step, we must move in the opposite direction with the forces of concern, persuasion, protest, non-cooperation, resistance, forgiveness, and kindness. Faith in Christ is to have faith in his path. His hope of a compassionate world of justice and peace becomes our hope as well.

In faith,
Ken Brown

Ken Brown is professor of philosophy and director of the Peace Studies Institute at Manchester College in Indiana.

LETTER NINE
Paul Grout

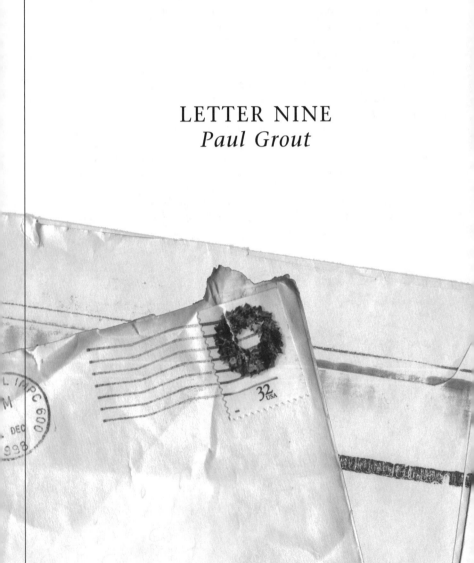

Dear sisters and brothers,

There is a saying in the Bible by Jesus that I think most people don't really understand: "Those who live by the sword, will die by the sword" (Matt. 26:52b). What that means may seem obvious; if we resort to violence we're going to get ourselves killed. But if it means exactly that, literally that, then it won't always be true. For instance, soldiers in a war often kill others without getting killed themselves.

Jesus doesn't mean that resorting to violence "sometimes" gets us killed. What he says is exactly true, in all circumstances, in every case; when we live by violence we die by violence. As soon as we begin to trust in violence to protect ourselves, something within us dies. What dies is that part of ourselves that Jesus came to save, that part that makes us truly alive, truly human—that part that can live on even after our physical death.

We live in a culture that has come to love "things" more than God or one another. We have become willing to trust in violence to keep our "things." The lives of other human beings have become expendable in maintaining our lifestyle. We have created weapons capable of killing millions of people to protect our lifestyle. No matter what political stand we may take on abortion, the deaths of millions of unborn babies destroy our souls. Because we live this way, we live every day in some form of fear. When we live this way, we are not alive as God intended us to be alive. There is a way to be fully alive—alive now and alive forever. There is a way of living at peace and unafraid. Jesus showed us that way; his life, death, and resurrection empowered that way.

When we receive the life that Jesus offers, we begin to understand that it can never really be taken away from us. Our lives become filled with love for every one and every thing that God has created. We begin to live unafraid, in thankfulness, in joy and awe. We feel in every moment that we are coming alive.

In peace,
Paul Grout

Paul Grout is an ordained minister, artist, and moderator of the 2002 Annual Conference.

LETTER TEN
Mary Sue (Helstern) Rosenberger

Dear Brethren youth,

For nearly three hundred years, Brethren have believed that "all war is sin and contrary to the will of God." Each generation—and each brother and sister—have witnessed to that conviction in their own unique way. Some have been martyred: Elder John Kline, Chandler Edwards, and Ted Studebaker. Some have suffered persecution or loss of property: John Naas and Christopher Sauer, Sr. Some have turned the other cheek nonviolently to the misunderstanding of their non-Brethren neighbors: Brethren who refused to carry weapons in World War I and congregations whose church houses were defaced with yellow paint for cowardice.

Some Brethren have expressed their peace witness in imprisonment or relocation: the Solingen Seven, Bob Gross, and those who moved to Canada to escape the draft. In every war, there have been great numbers of our Brethren ancestors who have acted out their peace testimony in prayer vigils and public protests. Many have witnessed through acts of helpfulness in times of warfare: the Brethren at Antietam, Brethren resettlement of dislocated Japanese-Americans, and hospital service and reforestation work through Civilian Public Service.

My generation's war was the Vietnam "conflict." Being female, I was not subject to the military draft as were my male friends and acquaintances. Still, the awful destruction and injustice of that undeclared war convinced me that I had to witness for peace in some small way.

I was inspired by the courage of those Brethren heroes of peace, my ancestors in the faith. I was motivated by family stories of those who served in alternative service and as "sea-going cowboys." So, in January 1966, armed with idealism and a brand-new nursing education, I went into Brethren Volunteer Service (BVS) and volunteered to go to Vietnam.

I arrived in Saigon in March and discovered a world totally different from anything I had experienced before! Asian hospitality, a complicated five-toned language, tropical heat, the predominant Buddhist religion, grinding poverty, refugees, and rice three meals a day were some of the reasons for my culture shock.

Far more difficult for me, however, was the culture created by war: prostitutes earning more than national legislators; taxi-drivers passing up their own people to pick up wealthy foreigners; the insecurity of land travel; every family touched by death at least once; bombed-out officers' quarters; civilian injuries from land mines; fatherless children roaming the city streets and girls as young as twelve learning to survive by selling themselves; endless traffic jams caused by two-and-a-half-ton military trucks on roads built for pedestrians and ox carts; and everywhere the destruction of a beautiful land and people by my own government!

At night, I could hear in the sounds of the shelling the truth of my ancestors' declaration that "all war is sin." I could see clearly in the light of the military flares that war is, indeed, "contrary to the will of God."

And you, my young brother, and perhaps my young sister, will need to make a choice when you reach the age of eighteen, the age of compulsory draft registration. Consider carefully, think clearly, and pray earnestly before choosing which way to go. The Prince of Peace invites you to follow and suffer for peace and goodness in creating a better world; the US military calls you to the use of power and force to help preserve the status quo.

Choose wisely, remembering that "all war is sin and contrary to the will of God." Let Selective Service know your convictions by writing a personal statement on the registration form before sending it in. Someday, when you must give an account of your faithfulness to future generations and to God, may you hear the words of approval, "Well done, good and faithful servant."

Continue the work of Jesus: Peacefully. Simply. Together.

Mary Sue (Helstern) Rosenberger

Mary Sue (Helstern) Rosenberger is an author, nurse, and retired chaplain at the Greenville (Ohio) Brethren Retirement Community.

LETTER ELEVEN
Mike Stern

REGISTRATION CERTIFICATE
This is to certify that in accordance with the
Selective Service Proclamation of the President of the United States

----
(First name)   (Middle name)   (Last name)

(Place of residence)
(This will be identical with line 2 of the Registration Card)

has been duly registered this _____ day of _____, 19____

(Signature of registrar)

Registrar for Local Board _____
(Number)   (City or county)   (State)

THE LAW REQUIRES YOU TO HAVE THIS CARD IN YOUR
PERSONAL POSSESSION AT ALL TIMES

D. S. S. Form 2
(Revised 6/9/41)   16—2163 ⊦

(Registrant must sign here)

Dear Brethren youth,

Walking up the aisle to the front of the church that Christmas Eve was possibly the hardest thing I had ever done. My palms were moist with sweat and my heart was pounding. The traditional midnight candlelight service was simple, yet rich with symbolism. A rustic manger scene behind the altar smelled of fresh straw and locally milled logs. We read the story of Jesus' birth. Everyone received an unlit white candle with a cardboard ring around it for catching the dripping wax. All the lights were to be turned off except for one candle. The flame would then be passed until each candle was lit. Every year it seemed that our flickering candles filled the room with more than any ordinary light.

Even though I had lived all of my eighteen years in that rural apple-growing community and I knew every face at that midnight worship service, there were no beckoning arms or welcoming smiles. Instead, our pastor's compact frame and jaw were firmly set. His lips pressed tightly together as I approached him. The slight shake of his head and the flash of anger in his eyes reiterated what he had said earlier: "Don't!"

"Why not?" I had asked. "I am in serious trouble and I need the prayers of my church community. In just two weeks, I could be facing up to five years in federal prison. I need to explain what I did, and this could be my last chance."

"Controversy will only divide the church," he answered. "I am not going to let you do this to us. Don't say anything. I won't allow it."

Even though I sincerely wanted his support and preferred not to disregard his wishes, I knew I had to speak. A pivotal moment had arrived and if I hesitated now, it would be gone forever.

During the closing stanza of "Hark the Herald Angels Sing," I walked with determination to the front of the sanctuary where the pastor appeared to be seriously considering the use of force to restrain me. I managed a smile and directly met his glare. As the song ended, I turned my back to him, faced the congregation, and said that my arrest and impending trial were the result of something they had taught me within these walls and in services like the one tonight.

~

Three months earlier harvest had been in full swing. Five of my closest friends were picking apples for my dad. Grant Verbeck and I were driving the tractors, hauling full bins out from the foliage and stacking them in rows for straddle trucks to carry to the packing house.

A reporter from the *Wenatchee Daily World* had called and said he was working on a story representing two views on the war in Vietnam. He had heard about my arrest and upcoming trial and wanted to know if I was willing to be interviewed.

"Of course," I said, "but during harvest we never quit till after dark. Can you come then?"

He met me at dusk two days later. My friends and Dad pulled up chairs in our cabin to listen to his questions and my responses. After the interview, the reporter turned to my father and asked, "Mr. Stern, how do you feel about what your son is doing?"

Never until this moment had I seen Dad cry. As his tears flowed and he choked back sobs, he said he was fearful for my safety and didn't want me to go to prison. But he said he was proud of me and he stood behind my decision.

~

Just one year earlier I was a seventeen-year-old senior in high school. It was 1970. Sparse facial hairs that I wanted to believe were the makings of a beard hinted at approaching manhood. I needed to distinguish myself from my parents and siblings, but the alternatives I saw around me didn't seem to fit. I wanted answers even though I had trouble formulating the questions. I was more fascinated and yet frightened by girls than I dared reveal to anyone.

Wondering if there was something wrong with me and the faith that I once thought I had, I was filled with questions, doubts, and unsolicited new truths that put many of my earlier beliefs on shaky ground. Moreover, I had acne, was skinny and uncoordinated, and probably had social skills to match. And I wanted these doubts and my acne to *just go away*.

But one major historical event was happening that would *not* just go away. It demanded my attention and necessitated a response whether I was ready or not. It was the war in Vietnam. All 18-year-old males were required by law to register for the draft and to kill or die, if called to do so. I had less than one year in which to make possibly the most important decision of my life.

In the midst of all other uncertainties, I felt increasingly sure of at least one thing: killing is wrong and if I was to continue calling myself a Christian, I could not go to war. I began to measure the wisdom and ethics of various conflicting viewpoints on the basis of this one certainty.

The most important influences in my life up to that time had come from people within the Church of the Brethren: my parents, older siblings, friends in the youth group, and a number of prophetic folks from around the country in the Brethren Action Movement (BAM). BAM was a group of articulate, passionate, and thoughtful individuals within the denomination who felt that our faith and religious tradition called us to radical discipleship in our personal lives and also in the corporate and political arena.

Specifically this meant nonviolent resistance to war and the arms race, engaging in the struggles for civil rights of minorities and women; being nonconformists in a society of affluence and over-consumption; respecting the environment; and identifying with the poor, the outcast and the powerless. In my search for answers, I looked in many places, but the responses from BAM folks always seemed the most meaningful and true to me.

As my eighteenth birthday came and went, I felt increasingly compelled not only to personally refrain from killing in Vietnam, but also to do something to stop the killing. I was uncomfortable with the moral implications of registering for the draft. If I were to register, wouldn't I be indicating acceptance of the government's authority to draft young men to war, forcing them into battle against others who perhaps had also been forced into battle? If I obtained conscientious objector status (as those with Brethren backgrounds easily could during that era), wouldn't I be shifting the burden of war's danger off my own shoulders and onto the less powerful or less articulate who were unable to obtain a similar deferment status? And wouldn't I be showing complicity toward the violence on all victims of war?

I decided to write an open letter to the draft board, the local press, and my denomination expressing my intentions and reasons for not registering. I hoped and believed that through clear and open witness to the power of nonviolent love I could be an instrument of change. The change I longed for would be an end to the war and a turning of hearts.

Before I completed the second quarter of my freshman year in college, an FBI agent who wanted to know of my whereabouts approached my parents. I dropped out of college and did some intense soul-searching, realizing that prosecution and prison could be imminent unless I changed the course I was on.

In a period of several months, my decision crystallized. The more certain it became that I was going to be prosecuted, the more certain I became that this was something I had to do.

I was arrested on September 19, 1972, and held overnight in the county jail in Wenatchee, Washington. I vividly remember looking out the window from the third story where I was being fingerprinted and seeing a group of my friends below on the lawn between the jail and the public library. They shouted and waved when they saw me and started singing "Hobo's Lullaby," a song I had often led the group in singing.

After a sleepless night, I was transferred to a bail hearing through a circuitous route, because the police feared another public display from the ten to fifteen rabble-rousing friends who had disturbed the peace by singing about it on the previous day.

The federal marshall who escorted me from jail to the hearing warned me that he was carrying a gun and was prepared to use it on me if I attempted to escape. When I asked him if he knew why I'd been arrested, he didn't seem at all interested.

At the bail hearing, Galen Miller, the minister of the Sunnyslope Church of the Brethren, several other leaders from the denomination who knew me from church camps and district youth activities, as well as my parents and friends, all came in a show of support. It didn't occur to me at the time, but they were probably not there just to vouch for my character and sincerity; they were also likely prepared to post bond to keep me out of jail. And I don't even know if they all agreed with me, at least in terms of how I had chosen to protest. I only know that they were there at a moment in time when it meant the world to me. Moreover, their presence demonstrated that my community of support was not limited to my scruffy and youthful contemporaries. It also included mature, level-headed business and community leaders, farmers, school board members, parents, and ministers. In the face of this unanticipated and respectable gathering, the judge decided to release me on personal recognizance without bail, as long as I promised to appear in court when a trial date was set.

The next three months until my trial were largely occupied with preparing my defense. Dale Brown (who was the 1972 Annual Conference moderator), Art Gish, my mom, and I all prepared to take the witness stand. By this time the draft lottery number that corresponded with my birth date had long since determined that I would not have been drafted to either military or alternative service as a conscientious objector, if only I would have registered. The prosecutor made several offers to drop the charges if I would just sign my name on the draft registration document, and he seemed baffled that I continued to refuse when the stakes were so high.

But I was thinking at the time about the stakes of complicity, which were too high to be ignored, so I stubbornly held my ground. I would not sign anything that demonstrated cooperation with the Selective Service System. The case went to federal court in Spokane, Washington, on January 16, 1973.

My trial was the most vivid spiritual experience I had ever had up to that point in my life. The defense we prepared was that I was not actually guilty of a crime, because my religious convictions prevented me from cooperating with any system of drafting young people to war. The law requiring registration for the draft was a violation of my religious freedom guaranteed under the Constitution. Indeed, it was the war (and the system of inducting civilians to become soldiers against their wishes) that should have been on trial, not me.

The prosecutor, Mr. Grey, maintained that this was an open and shut case based on the answers to just three questions. Did I know of the existence of a law that required eighteen-year-old males to register for the draft? Was I at least eighteen years old? And had I registered? The answers were completely clear, he said, and I was guilty. Moreover, he insisted that any defense testimony that related to anything other than these facts would bias the jury. He did not want them to know I grew up in a church that fostered pacifism and Christian discipleship, a denomination that had issued statements condemning all war as sin, and had urged their youth to either register as conscientious objectors or openly and nonviolently resist the draft, as I was doing. He did not want the jury to hear testimony from Dale Brown, the current moderator of the denomination, or from Art Gish or my mother who would testify that they all encouraged me from my earliest days to follow Jesus toward a way of peace, even in the face of persecution or prosecution.

Mr. Grey interrupted every single line of our defense with objections, and Judge Neill sustained almost every objection. We played a cat and mouse game for several hours even to suggest to the jury that moral and religious motivation was an issue. The prosecutor was even allowed to isolate the opening sentence of my letter to the draft board without allowing the jury to hear or see the rest of the letter as part of my defense. It started with my confession, "By refusing to register under the Selective Service Act, I am taking a definite stand." Probably the only uninterrupted space given to our defense was when I tearfully started reading the Beatitudes from the Bible. Only then did the prosecutor hesitate from his now familiar "Objection, irrelevant and immaterial" interruptions and the judge refrained from his "Sustained" rulings.

It was not until after the jury left to deliberate, with clear instructions to consider only what the judge and prosecutor had defined as the facts, that we were allowed an offer of proof from our defense witnesses, which was merely "for the record" in case of appeal. During this period with the jury out of hearing, we spoke freely.

Dale Brown began by telling a bit of Brethren history using the story of John Naas—who refused to be a soldier for the king of Prussia in spite of threats and torture. He then described the church's official position toward every war we have seen through history, and how Brethren generally opposed and refused to fight in them all.

Mom talked about her own and Dad's upbringing in the Church of the Brethren and her own feelings about war. She said she felt I was only following what I had been taught about a Christian response to war.

Art Gish articulated some principles of faith, which he had often shared with me as a friend and a counselor. He addressed the meanings of discipleship (to live what we believe), allegiance (to Christ, not Caesar), nonconformity, and the cross.

I simply explained why my Christian faith required registering my objections to war, which in this case meant *not* registering for the draft. It was much like one of the many worship services, BAM meetings, and youth conferences I had participated in over the past several years— except for one thing. We were in a federal courtroom and I might be taken directly to prison right after it was over for what I was saying. But I felt inexplicably uplifted and victorious, even in what appeared to be certain defeat in the courtroom. Indeed, even when the jury returned in less than an hour with its guilty verdict, I felt so sustained by God's hand that I was sure I would continue to be guided and protected, even if I went to jail.

But I was again released on my own recognizance, pending a sentencing date, and waited several more weeks before knowing my sentence: three years probation with a two-year work stipulation to do community service without pay. I initially expressed my desire to join Brethren Volunteer Service (BVS) to satisfy the conditions of probation, but the judge actually overruled any project associated with the Church of the Brethren. By that time he had concluded that our church focused so heavily on peace issues (and apparently promoted civil disobedience) that it must be incapable of providing legitimate community services. He also seemed to doubt the rehabilitative value of my further involvement in our denomination. However, Chuck Boyer (then director of BVS) helped me find a job in an inner-city Head Start center in Dayton, Ohio, where I lived in a house of BVS volunteers and completed the terms of probation. We just never informed the probation office of my continuing close connection to the Church of the Brethren or that I was spending most of my spare time promoting peace among local church youth groups.

~

People often ask me two questions when I tell them this piece of my life story: Would I do it again? And would I encourage my own children to follow a similar path? The short answer to both questions is yes. But the longer answer is that I could only do it again if I could muster some of the same courage and openness to accepting God's spirit and guidance that I had when I was eighteen and nineteen years old. And like my own loving parents, I would fear for the safety of my children if they chose to take this kind of risk to follow their conscience.

Nonetheless, I continue to say this to my children and to all youth whom I hope to touch with these words today. Wearing a uniform and following orders is no excuse for taking human life. No matter how justified or popular the cause might appear to be, I remain convinced that Jesus would not lead his followers into battle with weapons of war and destruction. Indeed, everything about Jesus points in a different direction.

War has come again, and there are strong indications that you personally will face difficult and costly choices in the very near future, whether you're ready or not. You must find your own way, of course, but it's definitely time to get ready. Some conditions have changed for better or worse, yet I think most of the key issues remain remarkably the same as they were thirty years ago. I pray for all of you and all of us—and for the sake of future generations—you will seek and find a way of peace.

Peace,
Mike Stern

Mike Stern is a registered nurse and a folksinger/songwriter from Seattle, Washington.

LETTER TWELVE
J. Kenneth Kreider

Dear young friends,

Despite the proclamation of "In God We Trust" on all our coins, most Americans support the president's reliance on military action in response to the events of September 11, 2001. While condemning members of Al Qaeda who slaughtered thousands of innocents in this country to get us to change our foreign policy, most Americans are willing to overlook US military exercises that have slaughtered thousands of innocent men, women, and children in Afghanistan in order to change the policies of that country.

Now, where does this leave the Brethren? Traditionally and historically, the Brethren have been a "peace church." Along with the Mennonites and Quakers, the Brethren have reminded other Christians that Jesus taught that all humans are children of God and that we are to do good to all people—even those who do evil to us (Matt. 5:38-48). By example, Jesus taught that his followers should not resort to violence—even in self-defense. Although he had the power to call down legions of angels against those putting him to death, he did not. He died asking God to forgive those who had done and were doing great evil to an innocent man.

Those who claim to be Christians (or Christ-followers), therefore, cannot support the militaristic hype and atmosphere being enthusiastically promoted throughout the country by our government, television programs, radio call-in shows, motion pictures, newspapers, and magazines. We must reject the glorification of war and violence in our schools, political discussions, electronic "games," and elsewhere. We must speak out against a military budget larger than the military budgets of all our supposed "enemies" put together. We must speak out against the president's use of the September 11 tragedy as an excuse to increase our already obscene military budget. Excessive military spending is robbing medical assistance to the elderly; spending on education, especially in the inner cities; assistance to the unemployed; and funds to improve our environment. The president's proposed increase ($48 billion) is more than the total military budgets of every nation in the world. If Christians do not speak out against this sinful waste of resources while tens of thousands of children around the world are starving, they are not being faithful to the call of Christ.

It is not popular to criticize American foreign policy. The Bible tells us that many go down the easy, broad path with the masses, but few are faithful and take the unpopular narrow road. Jeremiah, Daniel, Amos, Jesus Christ, St. Francis, Lucretia Mott, Sojourner Truth, Martin Luther King, Jr., and many other saints were not popular in their own day. Only after their deaths did most people realize the significance of lives lived in faithfulness to God.

Of course, we are thankful to be able to live in this country where most of us have so many freedoms and privileges. But can we overlook the fact that much of our privilege is paid for by people living in abject poverty—with no apparent way to escape? Can we as true Christians, like Pilate, wash our hands, look the other way, and pretend we don't know what is going on?

One of the great things about democracy and living in this country is that there is no excuse for ignorance. Information is available. Read, be informed of the realities of the world in which we live. Be courageous and speak out in Christian love. Raise questions about the ethics and morality of what we do and support, both individually and as a nation. Raise these questions in family groups, dorm rooms, rap sessions, public meetings, and wherever you have the opportunity to confront the mindless acceptance of "my country, right or wrong." For some people the values and ideals of their nation and its political leaders shape their own, but Christians remember that their first allegiance is to Christ, whose teachings are the basis of their values and actions. A true Christian does not go along with the worldly crowd. The Christian's mission is to be faithful, to witness to the truth of Christ's message, and to serve one's neighbor. This is much easier said than done. It takes courage, conviction, knowledge, and faith. It is not pleasant to be seen as an oddball or called a traitor if we question the military acts or the spending priorities of our nation. Nevertheless, we need to break the cycle of violence.

Many youth wear bracelets with the letters WWJD—What Would Jesus Do? Can you imagine Jesus flying in a bomber dropping bombs on the people in Afghanistan—or anywhere else? Can you imagine Jesus flying an airplane into a building? No, and those who choose to follow Christ cannot do that or support those kinds of actions. Some of our youth are wearing a second bracelet with the letters AWOL, Another Way of Living, to remind themselves—and others—that Christians are guided by the teaching of Christ, not popular culture. What are you planning to do as you follow Christ's teaching and example?

Remember the old lesson posed by the question, "If you were put on trial on the charge of being a Christian, would there be sufficient evidence to convict you?" In what ways are you any different in thought, actions, and speech than those who do not profess to be followers of the Prince of Peace? May God bless you as you strive to be faithful to the teachings of Jesus Christ.

In his name,
J. Kenneth Kreider

J. Kenneth Kreider is professor emeritus, Elizabethtown College. He is the author of A Cup of Cold Water, *which documents the history of Brethren Service.*

LETTER THIRTEEN
Tim McElwee

Dear youth of the Church of the Brethren,

Many of the young people I think of today will not be alive by the time this letter is published. Ours is a dangerous world, characterized by warped priorities. We hear it all the time: young people are dying by the thousands in our country and by the millions worldwide. But we'd just as soon not be bothered with disturbing facts like these. And besides, what difference does it make that every three hours in the US a person under the age of twenty is a homicide victim? How does that affect me? Should it matter that every day in the US one person under age twenty-five dies from HIV infection? Or that, according to the UN, one child in ten in developing countries dies before his or her fifth birthday, and 325 million children worldwide have no schools to attend? Even if we do care about these problems, what difference can one person make?

Actually, we have an impressive history of individuals in the Church of the Brethren making a significant difference in the world. Dan West pioneered hunger relief efforts such as Heifer Project International (HPI). Today HPI is making it possible for hundreds of thousands of poor families to put food on their tables. West later helped to start Brethren Volunteer Service (BVS), a program through which essential needs of thousands more are met by the hard work and voluntary service of others. Following her experiences in BVS, Yvonne Dilling traveled to Honduras where she invested herself (and nearly lost her life) in response to the plight of refugees from war-torn El Salvador. She continues her work with the poor of Central America today.

You can make a difference too, even if you don't feel called to this kind of dramatic witness. Simply offering a word of peace or nonviolently resolving a conflict in our violence-prone world will make a difference. You can make the world a better place by reaching across social boundaries and helping others feel good about themselves. And you can get involved in faith-based, political action. US public policy cannot solve all of the problems mentioned above, but changes in our social, economic, foreign, and military policies can help to create a world with more justice and less violence. For example, the United States ranks last among developed countries in terms of percentage of the economy provided for international development (0.11%). At the same time, the president has asked Congress to approve a $400 billion military budget for 2003. If approved, this budget would amount to three times the *combined* military budgets of all potential US military adversaries. Our country is spending hundreds of billions of dollars on the military while 1.2 billion people live on less than $1 a day. These disturbing policies must change. It is the poor, those with little to no voice in the political process, who suffer the most from these distorted priorities. Our voices can make a difference. In 1977, the Church of the Brethren Annual Conference declared: "The church has specific responsibility to defend and respond to the rights and needs of the poor, the disadvantaged, and those with insufficient power to assure their rights."

We can create a world where human need is prioritized over increasingly destructive means of taking human life. We can form a society that substitutes hate and violence with respect and cooperation. Change of this kind can come about if enough ordinary citizens like you and me care enough to make a difference. It will seem naively optimistic to some, but sweeping societal change *has* taken place throughout history. The system of slavery was overcome through an international abolitionist movement. The military and economic systems that keep a small percent of the world population wealthy while millions struggle and die in poverty can also be overcome. But it will happen only if we act—only if we believe that we can make a difference.

During the 1992 election year, Congressman Barney Frank was interviewed by a television reporter whose questions made it clear that she was very disappointed in the performance of the US government. Before she completed her next question, Congressman Frank interrupted her by saying, "Look, I know where you're going with this question: The American people don't really care for any of the presidential candidates, the American people are sick of the US Senate, the American people are fed up with the US House of Representatives. Well let me tell you something, the American people are no bargain either!" Congressman Frank went on to lecture the reporter about the apathy of the US citizenry, about our tendencies to complain and yet remain politically inactive, and about our preference to drift into self-pitying despair rather than engaged social and political action. In short, he told the reporter—and he tells us today—if you don't like the way the government is performing, get involved! Care enough to make a difference. In this democracy, the people *are* the government; we elect representatives to carry out our political will. But we often don't hold up our end of the bargain.

Bread for the World reports that every year six million children die from hunger-related causes. If we're honest, we would have to admit that we'd rather not think about facts like these. But if we refuse to see the faces behind the numbers, we won't feel empowered to try to bring about needed changes. If we pretend not to see, we won't respond. If we won't be the voices for those without a voice, injustice and violence will continue to dominate our world.

Mennonite theologian J. Lawrence Burkholder writes, "The cross of Christ is one that is imposed by the world upon those who confront the world and try to change it." How are you called to carry the cross of Christ?

Respectfully,
Tim McElwee

Tim McElwee is vice president for College Advancement at Manchester College and assistant professor of political science.

LETTER FOURTEEN
William Stafford

William Stafford was born in Hutchinson, Kansas in 1914. He taught at Lewis & Clark College in Oregon, was Poetry Consultant to the Library of Congress (1970–71) and Oregon Poet Laureate in 1975. He was a conscientious objector during World War II and served in Civilian Public Service (CPS) under the sponsorship of the Brethren, Quakers, and Mennonites. Stafford gives special tribute to the Church of the Brethren for its influence on his life. This chapter from his little book, Down in My Heart, *tells about CPS volunteers being mobbed by angry townsmen in Arkansas who hated them for what seemed like cowardice.*

When are men dangerous? We sat in the sun near the depot one Sunday afternoon in McNeil, Arkansas, and talked cordially with some of the men who were loafing around in the Sabbath calm. Bob was painting a watercolor picture; George was scribbling a poem in his tablet; I was reading off and on in *Leaves of Grass* and enjoying the scene.

When are men dangerous? It was March 22, 1942. The fruit trees at the camp farm were in bloom. We had looked at them as we went by, starting on our hike, and we stopped while I took a picture of George and Bob with our two little calves. We spoke of the war and of camp and of Sunday as we hiked through the pine woods and past the sagging houses. We knew our way around; we had done soil conservation work during our months in camp, in the fields beside our path. Not all had been friendly, it is true. Our project superintendent had warned us against saying "Mr." and "Mrs." to Negroes, and we had continued to use the terms; and one stormy night when no doctors would come out, some of the men in camp had given first aid to a Negro woman, whose husband had led them through the dark woods to the cabin where the woman lay screaming. Thus we had become friends with some of our neighbors. With some of them we had made friends, but it was harder with others, and we went to town inconspicuously, with care, no more than two at a time; and we were in most ways the quiet of the land, and unobserved, we thought.

When we had hiked into McNeil we had found a few men loafing around in the shade. The stores were closed; Main Street extended a block each way from the depot and then relaxed into a sand road that wandered among scattered houses. We too relaxed for our Sunday afternoon. Bob set up his drawing board; George got out his tablet and pen; and I sat leaning against a telephone pole and began to read—among dangerous men.

It takes such an intricate succession of misfortunes and blunders to get mobbed by your own countrymen—and such a close balancing of good fortune to survive—that I consider myself a rarity, in this respect, in being able to tell the story, from the subject's point of view; but just how we began to be mobbed and just where the blunders and misfortunes began, it is hard to say. We might have lived through a quiet Sabbath if it had not been for Bob's being an artist; or, especially, if it had not been for George's poem; and on the other hand we might have become digits in Arkansas's lynching record if Walt Whitman had used more rhyme in his poetry.

About eight of the townsmen gathered to look over Bob's shoulder as he painted. His subject was a dilapidated store across the street. The men were cordial and curious. I asked them questions about their town. The only time we were abrupt was when they asked where we were from. "Magnolia," Bob said, and quickly changed the subject to their town baseball team. One of the onlookers edged up behind George and looked over his shoulder, while George went on with his composing and revising—unheeding.

I went back to my book, and I'll never be able to remember whether I was reading, when it happened, "Come, I will make the continent indissoluble. . . ."

I looked up. The onlooker, a handsome young man, well-dressed, and with tight skin over the bridge of his nose, had snatched George's poem and was reading it.

"What's the idea of writing things like this?" he challenged. "If you don't like the town, you haven't any right to come around here." I was familiar with the edge on his voice. He knew we were COs.

George stood up, straight, with his arms hanging at his sides, his face composed, and remonstrated that he hadn't meant the poem to be read—he was just trying to write, trying to express his own feelings.

"Here," George said, "I don't want the poem; I'll take it and throw it away." The young man held the poem away from George's outstretched hand and took his discovery a few steps away to show it to another townsman. The two muttered. The first man returned. He scrutinized Bob's drawing, while George and I stood without moving and Bob went on painting—a little faster. What could we do when men were dangerous?

The young man spoke, not directly to us but to the other townsmen, some of whom had drawn nearer, about our being COs. There was more muttering, in which we began to hear the quickening words—"yellow" and "damn." At first these words the men said, about us, to each other;

then the faces were turned more our way when the words were said. A short, strong man broke into action, went to where Bob was still sitting, and grabbed the drawing board.

"Why, sir!" Bob said, and looked up as if in surprise.

"We'll take care of this," the short man said. He started to rip the drawing paper from the board, but another man stopped him.

"Save that for evidence." The short man raised the board over his head to break it over a piece of iron rail set like a picket near the depot; then he stopped, considered, caressed the board, and settled down to hold it under his arm and to guard the evidence.

"We ought to break that board over their heads," someone suggested. Several others repeated the idea; others revised the wording, expanded the concept, and passed the saying along. Some spoke of "stringing them up."

George got constructive. "I guess I'll go home," he said; "I don't think they like me here." He started to leave the circle—by now there were about fifteen men around.

"Hey, you; you're not going any place," one said.

"Don't let him leave," said another.

George came back and sat down.

A man at the edge of the group—a beautiful man to us—said, "Let's call the sheriff." This call was in turn echoed around. To our great relief someone actually crossed the street to call. The tension, however, was far from ended.

The young man who had started the inquisition turned to me. "What were you doing?"

"I was reading a book." I held it up—*Leaves of Grass*. "A poetry book."

"What's that in your pocket?" he asked, pointing to my shirt pocket. I explained that it was a letter which I had written.

"But you said you hadn't written a letter," he accused. The group of men shifted their feet. I explained that I had been reading a book immediately before, but that earlier I had written a letter. The questioner demanded it, arm outstretched. The others were watching these exchanges, sometimes retiring to the edge of the group to talk and then elbowing back. By now about twenty-five were present.

The questioner considered and then accepted my suggestion that he wait for authority before taking the letter. He turned away, and he and others tried to argue with George about his convictions on war. George wouldn't say much—just that he considered war the wrong way of attaining ends many agreed to be good.

Then the young man veered, in the midst of the discussion of war, to an accusation that George's writing was not poetry. There was an implication that if it wasn't poetry it might be something else—like information for the enemy. George said that he thought what he had written—it was being circulated constantly through the crowd, exciting rumbles of anger wherever it passed—was poetry, and that poetry didn't need to rhyme. This opinion brought snorts from the crowd. The young man said that poetry always rhymed. *Leaves of Grass* throbbed under my arm, but I said nothing.

Drawing down one side of his mouth and looking sideways at George, the young man said, "Where did you go to school?" He grabbed the book from under my arm and opened it at random. He read a passage aloud to the lowering group, to prove that poetry rhymed. He started off confidently, read more and more slowly, and finally closed the book with a snap.

"Well, that may be poetry," he said, "but what you wrote ain't." The crowd was a little taken aback. It shifted its feet.

By this time I had a chance to look over a shoulder and read George's poem, which I hadn't yet seen. It certainly was unfortunate—a Sandburgian description of McNeil beginning, "McNeil! Hmph! Some town, McNeil. . . ." An alert bystander clucked at a line in the poem: "And loaded freighters grumble through at night."

"There!" he said. "That's information. That's them troop trains!" We lost all we had gained from Whitman.

By this time, though, some of the group were arguing about why Bob painted. None of them could understand his insistence that he painted for fun. "But what are you painting that for?" they asked, pointing to the old store building. "It must be for a foreign power," one said.

"I don't think a foreign power could use a picture of this store in McNeil," Bob said. The chief prosecutor bristled.

"That's just where you're wrong, Bub—it's little towns like McNeil that's the backbone of the country, and Hitler knows it."

Bob was stunned by the contextual force of the remark; he was silent.

During all of this heckling and crowding we were merely quiet and respectful. We didn't know what else to do. We learned then rapidly what we later learned about other provokers—including policemen—that almost always the tormentor is at a loss unless he can provoke a belligerent reaction as an excuse for further pressure or violence.

Every few minutes a car would come to a stop near us to spout out curious people. The news was getting around; later we discovered that towns five or ten miles away had begun to hear about the spies almost as soon as the group began to form around us. The people of Arkansas stood off and talked, nodding their heads and reading—with more interest than most poets can hope to arouse—George's blunderbuss of a poem.

Finally, to our great relief, the police car from Magnolia rolled up. A policeman was driving; a man in plain clothes, who turned out to be a Federal revenue man, was beside him. The policeman gave us the first friendly word in a long time.

"That your work?" he asked Bob, nodding toward the picture still held by the evidence man. "That's pretty good."

The two representatives of the law took over, got our names, and gravely considered the indictments of the crowd. My letter was brought to light by the surrounding chorus of guards. The revenue man read it carefully, the onlookers craning over his shoulder. He retired to a new group. They read it. The officers took my camera, which had been confiscated by our guards, for evidence. They took *Leaves of Grass*. The policeman came back to the car, where we were standing. He was the first man we had seen in a long time who didn't either stare at the ground when looked at or glare back.

The revenue man circulated around through the crowd for at least half an hour, talking to local leaders. The mob at its greatest numbered not more than sixty, or possibly seventy-five. All assurances given, the revenuer came back to the car; and our two rescuers—our captors in the eyes of the mob—whisked us back to camp, where we created a sensation as we rode down past the barracks in the police car.

The mob scene was over; our possessions were returned to us—except for the picture, the poem, and my letter, which were placed on exhibit at the Magnolia police station to satisfy inquirers that all precautions were being taken. At camp we doubled the night watch, for fear of trouble; but nothing happened.

And the next morning, before work, we three stood before the assembled campers—about one hundred men, clothed in various shades of denim and of bits from the ragbag, and seated on long wooden benches—and gave our version of what had happened, in order to quiet rumors and to help everyone learn from our experience. The argument about poetry got a big laugh, as did Bob's "Why, sir!" Before leaving that barracks hall we had to talk over the mobbing thoroughly; for it signified a problem we had to solve: When are men dangerous? How could we survive in our little society within a society? What could we do?

For that occasion, our camp director, a slow-talking preacher of the way of life taught by Jesus Christ, gave us the final word:

"I know you men think the scene was funny, in spite of its danger; and I suppose there's no harm in having fun out of it; but don't think that our neighbors here in Arkansas are hicks just because they see you as spies and dangerous men. Just remember that our government is spending millions of dollars and hiring the smartest men in the country to devote themselves full time just to make everyone act that way."

We remembered, and set out to drain more swamps and put sod in more gullies in Arkansas.

This passage from Down in My Heart *is reprinted with permission of the Estate of William Stafford.*

LETTER FIFTEEN
Chris Douglas

Dear Brethren youth,

When the recent war in Afghanistan began after September 11, youth in the Sunday school class I help teach became aware of how different they were from many of their friends at school. While others were applauding the bombs being dropped in cities and villages of Afghanistan, youth from my congregation were horrified at the loss of innocent lives of men, women, and children. In our Sunday school class, we spent many weeks talking about the war, about how to make peace, about how difficult it is to be "different" from the values of the culture in which we live.

A number of years ago, the Church of the Brethren began using a slogan to describe itself: "Another Way of Living." In times of war, we become especially aware that Brethren understand the message of Jesus— the call to "another way of living." Revenge and retaliation are tempered by the call to love our enemies and to pray for those who persecute us. Forgive (even our enemies), in order that we might be forgiven. It runs counter to all that we hear from our politicians and in other messages from our society.

Romans 12:2 tells us, "Don't be conformed to this world," or in the words of *The Message*, a paraphrase by Eugene Peterson: "Don't become so well adjusted to your culture that you fit into it without even thinking. Instead, fix your attention on God. You'll be changed from the inside out. Readily recognize what he wants from you, and quickly respond to it. Unlike the culture around you, always dragging you down to its level of immaturity, God brings the best out of you, develops well-formed maturity in you."

It isn't easy to march to the beat of a different drummer when peer pressure and cultural values try to convince us that violence is the way to resolve conflicts. But for almost three hundred years, the conviction of Brethren has been that Jesus modeled for us another way of living, a way of justice and of peace. But how do we find the courage to march to the beat of a different drummer? My own experience suggests at least two important sources for that courage and strength: 1) reliance on God through prayer and worship, and 2) a community of sisters and brothers in the faith who stand with us, encouraging and challenging us.

The first source, reliance on God through prayer, was emphasized for me again recently when I visited the Taizé Community in France. I was reminded how important the resource of prayer is to the work of reconciliation and justice. Prayer sustains us in our efforts to keep trying, even when the odds feel overwhelming. The second source, community, is also imperative for me. I am a part of a small group in my congregation. We meet every other week and talk about our lives. Sometimes we challenge each other when one of us is tempted to become just another non-thinking member of this consumer culture who focuses only on "me." How important having that support and challenge is!

As the staff person for Youth/Young Adult Ministry for the past seventeen years, I have tried to facilitate ways that Church of the Brethren youth from all across our denomination can come together and support one another in the ways of peace. Events like National Youth Conference, workcamps, and Christian Citizenship Seminars are places to go to find other young people who are trying to follow Jesus in "another way of living." These are places where we encourage each other to find the things that make for peace.

My prayer for each young person in the Church of the Brethren is that your journey as a peacemaker will be strengthened by the resources of prayer and community.

Grace and peace,
Chris Douglas

Chris Douglas is coordinator of Youth/Young Adult Ministry, Church of the Brethren General Board.

LETTER SIXTEEN
Frank Ramirez

RK JOHNSON
- South Polp Way
.bec, CA 9-WS73

Dear Brethren youth,

I still have my old letter jacket from high school in the closet. It's black, with an A for Azusa. The year was 1972, and for many of us there was one thing on our minds. Nobody wanted to be in the last body bag coming home from Vietnam.

We were still getting used to the breakup of the Beatles in 1972 and wondering what it all meant. The Apollo program was winding down, but the nightly news still included the casualty count from Vietnam.

Watergate was barely on the horizon. There were race riots, assassinations, and civil turmoil, and a distrust in government and a war that never seemed to end. We were a generation raised on the honor and glory of war, but we were coming to grips with the fact that this war was going very badly.

I don't know if you've ever heard of a little thing called the draft lottery. Basically, government officials put the days of the year on slips of paper and put the slips in a big drum. Then they drew the dates out one by one. If your birthday was drawn first, you'd be drafted without a doubt. A high number and you'd almost certainly not be drafted. Mine was 31. I figured I was going to Vietnam too.

Decisions, decisions. Some people simply left the country. Some did not register and waited for the consequences. Some allowed themselves to be drafted or they volunteered. Some registered as conscientious objectors (COs) and went into alternative service. This has nothing to do with patriotism. We took our freedom seriously. And I knew as an Hispanic that our family had been given opportunities to succeed. I decided it was appropriate to register as a CO and to serve in alternative service.

The paperwork was a little difficult. I struggled because I wasn't sure about the biblical basis of nonviolence and didn't know there were Christian communities that would support me.

Fortunately, God is always busy. Never having heard of the Church of the Brethren and knowing nothing about the Brethren stance, I registered for my freshman year at La Verne College, a Brethren college. My first job on campus was in the dishroom of the cafeteria, where I fell in with several Brethren students.

I caught a real break. Mine was the first class whose draft numbers were not called. We heard the term "peace with honor," which basically meant that Nixon wasn't going to continue a war begun by the Democrats, and he was planning to pull our troops out of Vietnam one way or another. So basically I had it easier than most. I had made a decision to be a CO without having to follow through with action. My college education continued uninterrupted; I joined the Church of the Brethren and learned to love and appreciate our peace stance.

I learned that during World War I Brethren of high school and college age were encouraged by some leaders to refuse military service, but those very same leaders recanted when threatened with imprisonment by the government. In the end it was the young people who went to prison, sometimes suffering mistreatment or even torture. I learned that those same young people took things into their own hands to make sure the next generation would have guidance and support for their peace position. Those new leaders worked with the government to establish alternative service. If you want to read about heroes, there's a lot to discover about those who worked in mental hospitals and helped reform the system; those who volunteered for starvation experiments and became living skeletons; and those who helped pioneer the techniques of smoke-jumping, parachuting into the midst of national forests to fight fires. Some were guinea pigs in drug tests. These heroes served our country with glory and honor, and their story is worth relearning. Some of these young people are now eighty years old, but when I talk to them about their time of service, they look back with pride on having the opportunity to remain true to their faith while serving their country.

Well, it's your turn. I don't know what's going to happen. Neither do you. But it's important for you to know the basics and basis of Christian peacemaking. After all, we're not pacifists—not if it means being passive while others are hurting. We actively "seek peace and pursue it."

Peacemakers don't believe that everyone is sweet and nice. We don't believe in the way of peace because it's easier, or safer. The way of peace is harder than the way of the world. No, the reason we practice peace is that we want to follow Jesus. We don't follow Jesus because he gives us some convenient reasons to get out of serving in the military. We serve Jesus first and foremost, and the price of this discipleship leads us on the more difficult path.

I spoke recently with a college-aged woman who served with Christian Peacemaker Teams in Colombia; while there she was confronted by masked gunmen along the riverside. Her known commitment to peace brought the gunmen into dialogue with villagers who feared them. That's bravery. That's making a difference in the world.

You have many opportunities to be a peacemaker. You don't have to wait for war or a draft. But you should know why you are against war. You should be able to tell others. And you should have the courage to stick to your guns—I mean principles.

Here's something important as well. I hope you will respect the opinions of others, especially if you want them to respect your choice. I grew up in a military family, and I know that people who serve in the military are not evil. They believe that what they are doing is right, just as you believe what you are doing is right. Be sure to understand why we are for peace. It is because of the way of Jesus.

I remain Christ's servant and yours,
Frank Ramirez

Frank Ramirez is an author and pastor of the Everett Church of the Brethren in Everett, Pennsylvania.

LETTER SEVENTEEN
Wayne Zunkel

To all who are called to "mission impossible,"

All of us who name the name of Christ are "called to an almost impossible mission." Even though our neighbors and our nation's leaders may be focused on war and violence, we are called to find simple ways to live the love of God toward those perceived to be the enemy. This may be a difficult and dangerous task.

War requires an almost seamless, uniform hatred toward those perceived to be the enemy. To stand in the way of this is to draw withering fire, as some Church of the Brethren youth in Indiana discovered after they declined to wear shirts with a patriotic message as a show of unity for a war effort. These kids would tell us that "peace takes guts." Peacemaking requires an open heart, a clear mind, and a bundle of courage.

Peacemaking does not require a detailed response to the elaborate plans of war. It does require an intelligent, creative, and courageous response.

Glenn Smiley, one of the people who taught Martin Luther King, Jr., about nonviolence, was asked to talk to elementary school students in South Central Los Angeles. Every child in that class had witnessed somebody meeting a violent death. Smiley talked to them about how to react in a violent situation. The children decided that one should "do something different" when confronted with possible violence. Smiley used the illustration of a woman with a load of groceries in each arm crossing a nearly empty parking lot behind a supermarket at dusk. She heard footsteps behind her. As she walked faster, the footsteps quickened. As she walked slower, they slowed. She walked to the trunk of her car, then turned around and faced the man who was following her. In her softest, gentlest voice, she said, "Would you mind holding these bags of groceries for me?" She handed him her full grocery bags, then unlocked the trunk of her car and said, "Thank you so much." She took back the groceries and put them in the trunk of her car, closed the trunk, went around and unlocked her car, and drove away.

After the Los Angeles policemen who had beaten Rodney King were found "not guilty," parts of the city erupted in burning and violence. People were afraid to enter the riot area. A truck driver passing through the area was pulled from his truck and beaten by angry onlookers. He happened to be in the wrong place at the wrong time. Following the unrest Edward James Olmos, the actor who played the teacher in

Stand and Deliver, went alone to the epicenter of the riots carrying only a broom. Early on a Sunday morning, he quietly began to sweep up broken glass from storefront windows. That simple act of caring spoke volumes to a city paralyzed by hatred and fear.

Caution: Living love in the face of anger can cost you your life, as many peacemakers, including Jesus, could tell you.

When Soviet President Mikhail Gorbachev announced that he was no longer a Communist, Soviet tanks filled Red Square facing the Presidential Palace. A Russian woman phoned many of her friends. She asked each friend to phone other women asking them to join her in Red Square bringing cookies, candy, and cigarettes. When the square was filled with women, one by one each walked up and knocked on a tank and asked, "Have you come to kill your mothers and your sisters?" When a soldier looked out of his tank, he was given a gift of candy, cookies, or cigarettes. One by one, the tanks backed up and drove away into the night.

A similar experience happened in the Phillippines when Dictator Ferdinand Marcos negated Corazon Aquino's election as president. Marcos was trying to overturn Aquino's victory. Philippine women brought bouquets of flowers in addition to cookies and candy to the tank drivers who were filling the streets. The tanks withdrew.

A pastor in East Germany invited his people to come to the church one evening a week. They prayed for deliverance from East German communist rule and sang hymns; then each, holding lighted candles, stood outside in silence. At first there was a handful of worshipers, then hundreds. Eventually they surrounded the church. East German police were ordered in to disperse the worshipers. But when the police saw worshipers holding lighted candles in silence, they refused to disburse unarmed, peaceful people. The grip of the East German police was broken.

When you are confronted with possible violence, do something different. One solitary life can make a big difference if steadfastly dedicated to truth and love in the midst of an ocean of hate and fear. In your research, study well the peace pioneers such as frail Gandhi standing alone against the mightiest power of his day, Great Britain. Study Mexican American Cesar Chavez among downtrodden farm workers in the San Joaquin Valley of California. Study Nelson Mandela in a South African prison as he later forgave his guards and brought whites and blacks into one government. Study Lech Walesa, who led the common workers to freedom in Poland. Study Martin Luther King, Jr., as a young pastor serving Dexter

Avenue Baptist Church, a block down the street from the Montgomery, Alabama, state capitol where segregationists ruled. Consider SueZann Bosler, a young Brethren woman who witnessed the murder of her father, Bill, and was herself attacked and left for dead. She worked for years to save her father's killer from the death penalty. Study Pastor Martin Niemoller standing alone against Adolph Hitler. Study Ted Studebaker and Chandler Edwards, young Brethren volunteers who gave their lives living the way of love in Southeast Asia during the Vietnam War. Reflect on the lonely journey of Dennis Lipton, the US Air Force physician who repaid what the Air Force had spent on his medical training and then was court-martialed as he sought release from the military as a conscientious objector. Study Jesus of Nazareth, who set his face steadfastly toward Jerusalem to die, forgiving those who killed him.

Study well, and sign onto Jesus' seemingly "mission impossible."

Blessings on your journey,
Wayne Zunkel

Wayne Zunkel is a retired pastor and former editor of the Brethren Peace Fellowship newsletter.

LETTER EIGHTEEN
Brian Lahman Yoder

Dear friends,

As a teacher, I am privy to the minds of children and youth. Today as we discussed their latest current events assignment, I heard two boys in my class openly express their desire to "take a bomb and drop it on all the weaker countries—and one especially on Osama bin Laden." One of the boys went on to say, "I think we should have another world war just so we can wipe out the threats against us."

Surprisingly (or not), nobody in the class offered other suggestions for solving the world's pain and suffering. As I glanced around at the other students, some of them were looking away awkwardly, many were fiddling with papers at their desks, and others were whispering irrelevant rumors to their friends.

Initially, I felt angry—I could feel my blood starting to boil, and I wanted to argue with the boys and debate the issue with the class. And just as quickly, I felt discouraged. How can I be a witness for peace among youth who find the details of war so minimal that they would be willing to launch a third world war? What will it take to open the eyes of our youth to see the destruction that they have the *luxury* of not witnessing each and every day?

Then I remembered all of you—you peace-loving, joy-sharing, love-abiding Church of the Brethren youth, who so desperately need to speak your truth to these friends at school and at work. I implore you to live your lives in reverence to God, in ways that Jesus would, so that your parents, teachers, and employers can be renewed by your eternal optimism and strength. It may seem like a daunting task, but I know you are up to the challenge. Put the anger, gossip, and ignorance of peers away and start spreading the vision of world peace!

God's peace,
Brian Yoder

Brian Lahman Yoder is a teacher in Peoria, Arizona, and is a past coordinator of National Youth Conference.

LETTER NINETEEN
George Dolnikowski

When the Soviet Union was invaded by Germany in World War II, George Dolnikowski was wounded and captured. His German captors suspected George was a spy when they discovered he could speak the German language, but instead of killing him they forced him to work as an interpreter. In his book This I Remember, *Dolnikowski recalls the good that was accomplished through the kindness of a few people and the power of forgiveness, despite the horrors of war.*

After the war, Dolnikowski was one of thousands of "displaced persons" resettled in the United States by the Brethren Service Commission. He became a student at Juniata College and did graduate work at the University of Pennsylvania before returning to Juniata as a professor.

The following is an excerpt from This I Remember *(1994, Brethren Press), in which he tells about a time he was in prison and a German officer forced him to clean mud from the officer's boots.*

I remember the day when Joanne and I were appointed to a position of directors of the Brethren Colleges Abroad Program in Marburg, Germany.

We traveled on a German boat, the *Bremen*, in July 1970. The night before we were to arrive in Germany, I could not sleep. The past was so alive in me again. A German boat, a German servant, the German language … There I was, returning to a country where I'd spent so many days in prison.

And suddenly I thought of the sergeant. I remembered his name and that he came from Frankfurt. I began thinking, I'll settle in Marburg. Then I'll go to Frankfurt and do everything possible to find the sergeant. What if I find him? What will I do? I will go to a place where I can make my shoes muddy, I will throw them in front of him and say, "There. Clean them and polish them." What if he refuses? I will buy a pistol. If he refuses, I'll kill him.

With all these thoughts in my head, I couldn't sleep all night. In the morning, when we got up, Joanne asked, "Why are you so pale? You look so tired."

I told her I didn't know.

Then I opened the door and there were my shoes. The servant had polished them without my even asking. I was so amazed. A German had polished my shoes! I thanked God.

Suddenly I smiled. The burden of all the memories that had accumulated during the night had been relieved. Joanne saw my smile and asked what had happened. I told her that it was a beautiful day.

Now when I polish shoes at home and people compliment us, Joanne says, "Oh, George likes to do that." People ask me if that's true and I say, "Yes, especially for those whom I love."

LETTER TWENTY
Debbie Roberts

Dear youth,

I remember when I first heard about the Church of the Brethren. I was eighteen years old and a freshman in college. I had been active in various churches all my life—Presbyterian, Baptist, and Methodist. Conversations I had that year with Brethren students were the first time I heard the words *peace* and *Jesus* in the same sentence. I remember feeling like I had come home.

As a young person during the Vietnam War, connecting faith to active peacemaking was crucial for me, and it still is today, more than thirty years later, in the midst of the fear and retribution following the crisis of September 11. Today, as I write this, Israel Defense Forces are overtaking the city of Bethlehem, a city that symbolizes the literal roots of our Christian tradition, but a city that is home also to many Muslim and Christian Palestinians. The world is witnessing a political struggle in which religion is often used as a justification for violence, a level of violence that often is not possible without financial support. For decades the United States has supplied the Israeli government with billions of dollars. This money has provided an avenue for the brutal and illegal occupation of the West Bank and Gaza, which has in turn led to razing homes, cutting down ancient olive groves, and repressing the rights of Palestinians.

When I was licensed to the ministry in a small country church in the Midwest, the congregation gave me a manual for Brethren ministers, a certificate to celebrate my licensing, and a newspaper. The newspaper was especially meaningful because the message it conveyed was that my pastoral responsibility included keeping up on current events. In other words, Christian faith calls one to respond to what is going on in the world. Where there is hatred, we are called to sow love. Where there is injustice, we are called to sow justice. We share this world with people of many ethnicities, cultures, and faiths. Affirming that *Jesus* and *peace* belong in the same sentence reminds us again and again of the importance of learning to know and respect each other with our hearts, souls, and minds. And, when we find respect lacking, we are to confront it—nonviolently but actively.

I long for people of faith to speak with clarity and vision regarding our responsibility for peacemaking in this world. I long for all of us to insist on justice for those who suffer at the hands of others, whether they be individuals, whole communities, or nations. I long for you, the youth of our denomination, to be bearers of our rich peace heritage in a spirit of love, openness, and service to all our brothers and sisters in the human family. Finally, I long for you to be supported in your commitment to peace-making, as I was, by peers and adults who will talk with you about your questions, walk with you as you live out your commitment, and pray for you as you struggle to remain faithful to your calling. May you find a home in peacemaking.

In a spirit of hope and gratitude,
Debbie Roberts

Debbie Roberts is campus minister and director of Peace Studies and Summer Service Programs at the University of La Verne in California.

LETTER TWENTY-ONE
Cliff Kindy

Dear younger sister and younger brother in the Church of the Brethren,

I am writing to you as I load my backpack for another assignment with Christian Peacemaker Teams (CPT) in one of the militarized conflict zones of the world. My wife, Arlene, just came home from her women's Bible study of Esther asking, "What are you willing to die for?" Well, I have had an M-16 up against my chest when Israeli soldiers burst into the Palestinian home I was visiting in Rafah Refugee Camp in the Gaza Strip. I have been accosted by armed paramilitaries and guerrillas on the isolated mountain trails of Colombia. And I have been arrested in a major military operation for being part of a nonviolent resistance camp in the US bombing zone of Vieques, Puerto Rico. I am, at times, willing to risk my life in an ongoing witness for justice and for peace.

Today the United States tries to defend its killing of others on the grounds they are terrorists. I urge you not to obey orders to kill. Whatever the justification, it is not more important than Jesus' words: "Love one another as I have loved you" (John 13:34).

As we grapple with the issues of discipleship to Jesus, does our allegiance belong to this Jesus we call Lord and Savior? Do we obey his orders or those that conflict with his way of love? Is he the one we trust to save us and give us security, or do we get security from our own power and military strength? We can't have it both ways.

We are in some difficult times now. Emotions are high because of fear and insecurity after the attack on the World Trade Center. Following Jesus in his way of peace can be pretty lonely, but there are thousands of others on that same pilgrimage.

Our Church of the Brethren has always done a good job of going in to fix things after wars. We care for the refugees of war. We send clothing and food for the victims of war. We help to rebuild after the destruction caused by war and violence. But do we have a role in preventing these wars? If so, we may need to be more alert and pro-active. Then we sure would save lots of postwar work! I have read the New Testament and understand that Jesus intervened in situations of injustice and violence before they grew larger (see Mark 5:1-20; note the demon possession by the "Legion" of the Roman occupation). How can we do that?

Jesus did this in spite of the threats and attacks he faced. The Easter resurrection was the affirmation that the nonviolent actions of God through Jesus are stronger than the powers of death. The powers of death have been defeated. The reign of God has overcome the forces of evil. Humanity is saved by God and reconciled to God (John 3:16-21 and 2 Cor. 5:16-21).

Jesus' words to us as disciples help us keep our "enemy" category small (see Matt. 5:25). Paul does the same with his counsel to "overcome evil with good" (Rom. 12:21).

The evangelism of the church on behalf of God's reign, which means getting folks to live as Jesus invites us to live (Matt. 28:20), probably has its most dramatic setting in the midst of the violence and injustice that build toward war. Do we as followers of Jesus have the boldness and vision that will be required for this task? Will you get in the Way?

Salaam/Shalom! (*Peace and wholeness* in Arabic and Hebrew)

Cliff Kindy

Cliff Kindy is an organic market gardener and a fieldworker for Christian Peacemaker Teams, a program supported by Mennonite, Quaker, and Church of the Brethren congregations.

LETTER TWENTY-TWO
Matt Guynn

Dear Cousin Michael,

"Today this scripture has been fulfilled in your hearing." These words from Luke 4 echoed in my head as I duct-taped my glasses to my face with trembling fingers, so that I wouldn't lose them if the dogs attacked.

I'd heard Susan Boyer preaching on this passage only a few weeks before, and today the words reassured me and brought me to trust.

I was standing in bright cold winter snow in northern Wisconsin, preparing to enter a US Navy base and reclaim it for the purposes of Life, cleansing it of killing and death. After climbing the barbed wire fence, we would encounter German shepherds that I could already hear barking, and I was terrified.

But those words from scripture kept ringing in my ears. They come at the beginning of Jesus' ministry. He starts things off by standing up in the temple and reading the scroll of Isaiah. He might have chosen any-thing, but he chose a passage that declares freedom to the oppressed and the forgiveness of debts (not sin, mind you, but monetary debts—that is the "year of the Lord's favor" part).

> *The Spirit of the Lord is upon me,*
> *because he has anointed me to bring good news to the poor.*
> *He has sent me to proclaim release to the captives*
> *and recovery of sight to the blind, to let the oppressed go free,*
> *to proclaim the year of the Lord's favor.*

Then he says: "Today this scripture has been fulfilled in your hearing."

Soon after I taped my glasses to my face, we walked toward the mil-itary base, shared in prayers and singing, and began to climb the fence. I was arrested at the top, with my glove stuck on the barbed wire.

Why do something like that? Because it's the "right" thing? To get into heaven?

Would you do it?

Ever since I was in high school, I have been aware that there is something more for us—more Life, more Wonder, more Passion. What brought me that day to climb the fence at the Navy base was that I have fallen deeply in love with life. That's what sustains, that love and caring so exemplified by Jesus.

I want you to know about Jesus—not only the Jesus you usually hear about in church, and definitely not the Jesus you hear about from the rest of society. I want you to know the Jesus who calls us into a life and relationship with him and with all of Life.

Read through the Bible and notice who Jesus hangs out with it. They are not the cool people. They are the ones without power, or the ones who are despised. Jesus calls us to a deep care and *compassion* ("passion-with").

Is the Jesus you love leading you to love the world more deeply? What are you doing about it?

Already I see you caring and wanting to actively stand up for Life, and already I see you receiving the small bruises that those of us who do care and love deeply have also received. As you follow Jesus more, you will love more, you will love more deeply, you will celebrate life more, and you will rise up with a song in your heart.

Life is not just about the NFL, NBC, CNN, NBA, and Nike. You already know that. I think you know that the "life" offered by these will not keep you alive. There is something more. Can you feel the "more" that I am writing of? It is underneath, around, and among us, singing through the noise of daily life.

I care so passionately about the world. I see God moving in amazing ways not as some Being dropping in and out to fix things, but as a constant Presence that we draw on and that flows through us. This Love, this God, whom I'm writing about, is the reason we stand up for peace and for Life in a different way—in *many* different ways.

Some of my response to this Greater Life has been like the story I started with. For a time, I worked in southern Mexico with an organization called Christian Peacemaker Teams, living in refugee camps with people whose lives were threatened. In September of last year I was there, keeping watch at night in the coffee groves outside the homes of people who feared violence against them, praying together with them in the candle-lit dark nights for peace and for spiritual nourishment.

But the scariest thing I have done recently took place in the grocery store near my home. As I was checking out, I raised the issue of the "war on terrorism" with the cashier and shared with her that I have a different opinion than most people, that I don't want more killing and bombing to happen, that I think any longer-term solution has to address the real causes.

It is scary to raise questions and to stand up for what I believe—it just doesn't feel safe. And it feels crazy. But Life pulls me out of my fear.

There are so many ways to testify to the Life that we see clearly. Far away or close to home, how are you falling in love with Life? And what are you being called to do about it?

With much love and care,
Matt

Matt Guynn is coordinator of the Seeking Peace project for On Earth Peace Assembly and has been coordinator of training for Christian Peacemaker Teams.

LETTER TWENTY-THREE
Maurice Hess

Maurice Hess was a young man at the beginning of World War I. As a member of the Old Order German Baptist Brethren, he refused to be drafted into the Army and was imprisoned in a military prison. Following is a portion of his court martial statement, which he crafted and preserved on a scrap of tissue paper. After recounting the details of his case, he said:

I do not believe that I am seeking martyrdom. As a young man, life and its hopes and freedom and opportunities for service are sweet to me. I want to go out into the world and do my work and make use of what little talent I may have acquired by long and laborious study.

But I know that I dare not purchase these things at the price of eternal condemnation. I know the teaching of Christ, my Savior. He taught us to resist not evil, to love our enemies, to bless them that curse us, and do good to them that hate us. Not only did He teach this, but He practiced it at Gethsemane, before Pilate, and on Calvary. We would, indeed, be hypocrates [*sic*] and be traitors to our profession if we should be unwilling to bear the taunts and jeers of a sinful world, and imprisonment, and torture, and death, rather than to participate in war and military service. We know that obedience to Christ will gain for us the glorious prize of eternal life. We cannot yield, we cannot compromise, we must suffer.

Two centuries ago our people were driven out of Germany by religious persecution, and they accepted the invitation of William Penn to come to his colony where they might enjoy the blessing of religious liberty which he promised them. This religious liberty was later confirmed by the Constitution of Pennsylvania and by the Constitution of the United States.

If those in authority now see fit to change those fundamental documents, and to take away our privileges of living in accordance with the teaching of the Scriptures of God, then we have no course but to endure persecution as true soldiers of Christ. If I have committed anything worthy of bonds of death, I do not refuse to suffer or die. I pray to God for the strength to remain faithful.

Brethren historian Donald Durnbaugh fills in the details of Hess's long ordeal in prison in his book Fruit of the Vine.

Hess was sentenced to imprisonment for life. Along with forty other COs, Hess was sent to the disciplinary barracks at Fort Leavenworth, Kansas, to begin his sentence. Because he could not accept commands given there to work—seeing no difference between accepting orders on a military base or in a military prison—he was thrust into solitary confinement. Some prisoners were shackled by their wrists to the bars of their cells in such a way that they could not support their weight by standing; Hess was chained with his hands just below the level of his shoulders. This lasted nine hours a day (for as long as other prisoners were working) and continued for 23 days until Secretary of War Baker outlawed the practice. His action came after news of the practice reached the outside press. Hess wrote his father shortly thereafter, saying, "There is much less probability of a physical breakdown now that they [the shackles] are no longer used."

…Hess's sentence had been reduced on review to 25 years but Hess was actually released in January 1919, along with others. After release, Hess taught for many years at McPherson College, recounting his wartime experiences when asked. Among his prison friends was one of the four Hutterites whose brutal treatment elicited some of the harshest criticism of the government's policies. Because they refused to put on military clothing in prison, they were treated so abominably that two of them died in captivity. As a final indignity their corpses were clothed in uniforms and sent to their families.

LETTER TWENTY-FOUR
Esther Mohler Ho

Hi there, gifted one! Yes, you with the glimmer in your eye and the edge of determination in your voice.

Probably you're upset, as I am, about the mess the world is in, about the uncontrolled violence and the corruption of the environment. Perhaps you also dream of "making a difference"—of helping to bring the loving, peaceful reign of God to the earth. Or possibly you're feeling overwhelmed by the situation and wondering if it isn't futile to even try to make changes. Whatever your current mood, I'd like to share with you my adventures in trying to walk God's path of love and reconciliation.

I was born seventy years ago on a farm in the southeast corner of Kansas. My primary social contact was the local Church of the Brethren, which I attended with my family almost every Sunday. There I heard many sermons and Sunday school lessons about living peacefully and being of service to others. When several Brethren Volunteer Service workers visited our church during my high school years, I decided that I would one day enter BVS. That dream came true after I graduated from McPherson College and taught school for two years. I was assigned to Kassel, Germany, to work as representative for the International Christian Youth Exchange. Even though I sometimes wondered what a simple Kansas girl with an all-too-limited command of the German language was doing in such an important role, I never seriously doubted that God had called me to that place and expected me to be an ambassador for peace. I began to realize that working for peace needed to be a major focus of my life.

Upon returning to the States, I accepted employment at our denominational offices in Elgin, Illinois. Working under Ralph Smeltzer, director of Peace Education and Action, I learned that Christians not only must live peaceably in their families and communities, but also must try to influence the way that our government treats people. Smeltzer also put his beliefs about the dignity of all people into action in the city and county in which he lived.

As my family and work responsibilities began to lessen, I joined the Ecumenical Peace Institute (EPI), a local faith-based peace and justice organization, which educates about the connections between militarism, racism, and poverty and leads the way in attacking these evils. Although some members of EPI had been practicing civil disobedience against unjust laws and actions of our government for many years, I didn't risk arrest until about ten years ago when the group decided to occupy a house that HUD (Housing and Urban Development) was placing on the market. According to the law, these "excess" properties were to be turned over to homeless or poor people. Instead, HUD was selling them for a large profit. Members of our group and several homeless people cleaned and repaired the house for homeless people to live there. In the wee hours of the morning, the police roused us and gave us the choice of leaving or being arrested. Most of us, feeling that we were on solid moral ground, decided to stay. We spent several hours in jail before being released. The courts took no action against us.

Once I had broken the "sound barrier" by being arrested, I found numerous opportunities to "put my body where my beliefs are," including several times at Livermore Nuclear Weapons Labs, once at the Navy's ELF Project facilities in Wisconsin, and this past fall at the School of the Americas in Fort Benning, Georgia, where our government has trained many Latin American military personnel in methods of torture, which they have used to commit atrocities against their people. My most recent arrest came at a "die-in" at the local federal building, commemorating the deaths of thousands of Afghanis caused by American bombing. I enjoyed carrying out my court-imposed sentence of six hours of community service by tutoring at a homeless shelter. My pastor commented that sentencing me to do community service was like sentencing an overeater to work at a candy shop!

Perhaps my most significant step for peace was deciding to join Christian Peacemaker Teams (CPT). The decision grew out of the frustration felt by many of us when war was raging in Bosnia. We knew that bombing was not the right answer, but we felt tongue-tied when people asked us what we would recommend. One evening a member of EPI astounded us by stating that he had written to the president suggesting that instead of bombing the country, we should send in a nonviolent peace force and that he would volunteer to be in the first group. Although I felt that I would not have the courage to join such a venture, the rightness of the idea seized my conscience.

I soon learned that the Church of the Brethren was involved in this kind of work through Christian Peacemaker Teams (CPT). Over the coming months, the nonviolent peace team idea continued to grow within me, and in December 1994, I entered CPT training. During my first summer I went to a high-crime area of Washington, DC. The following two summers were spent in Hebron on the West Bank, where we tried to reduce the violence between the Palestinians and the Israelis by being "human shields" and reporting on what we saw. I spent the next three summers with the CPT project in Chiapas, Mexico, where indigenous people are victims of a low-intensity war being waged against them by their government, with the backing of the US government. Last fall I spent two and a half weeks in New Brunswick, Canada, in solidarity with the native people who are attempting to exercise their treaty rights to fish for a living.

In addition to EPI, I am a member of the Interfaith Witness for Peace in the Middle East and co-chair of the Peace with Justice Commission of the Northern California Interreligious Conference. I serve as co-coordinator of the Congregational Peace Network of the Pacific Southwest District of the Church of the Brethren. Though the administrative tasks related to these responsibilities may not sound as thrilling as being "on the front line" in Hebron or Chiapas, I'm convinced that this work is every bit as important. In recent months, I have helped set up grassroots dialogue and action among different faith groups.

Over the years I've nurtured the fantasy occasionally that I could make a monumental breakthrough for peace in my lifetime, but most of the time the victories have been small ones. I've tried to focus simply on walking persistently in the pathway of peace and nonviolence and on being faithful to the calls that come to me. But it's been an exciting pilgrimage. My prayer is that you too will find yourself on a peacemaking trek. No one can give you exact directions as you venture out or tell you exactly where you will end up. Nevertheless, I urge you to step out boldly, trusting the Divine within and around you to grant you the wisdom and compassion needed for the journey.

His servant,
Esther Mohler Ho

Esther Mohler Ho is a retired teacher and a Christian Peacemaker Team reservist.

LETTER TWENTY-FIVE
Greg Davidson Laszakovitz

Dear youth,

When I reached the age of eighteen and had to decide whether or not to register with Selective Service, I faced a difficult decision. On one hand, if I did not register I could be certain of several things: I would not qualify for financial aid for college; I would be disqualified from government employment, limiting my future employment options; my father, as an ex-US Air Force mechanic, would go through the roof if he found out; and last but not least, I might appear a coward. On the other hand, I was taught that to kill was simply wrong, and I also learned that many Brethren had refused military service because it contradicted their beliefs as Christians.

The list of reasons to register was a lot longer than the reason not to register. But after much prayer, thought, and debate, it was with a shaky hand that I scrawled "conscientious objector" on the bottom of my Selective Service form. (There was, and still is, no prescribed space on the form to express the belief that war is wrong and that I will not kill another.) It was a small act of protest, but I felt like my action was a way to avoid getting into trouble with the law and, at the same time, let my government know that I am opposed to war. If I were drafted in a war, which didn't seem likely at the time, I could request that my card be pulled up and they would see I had registered and that as a Christian I was opposed to killing. There was no guarantee this would work in the event of a draft, but there weren't many options.

Soon after my eighteenth birthday (and filing my registration card), Iraq invaded Kuwait in the Middle East. This action prompted the United States to enter the fray and go to war. Some said it was in defense of Kuwait; others claimed it was to defend Kuwait's vast oil reserves that the US depended on to keep our cars on the road. Whatever the reason, my college dorm buddies and I began to wonder if a draft might be instituted and if we would be forced to fight.

Patriotism soon swept the campus. Many young men were excited by the thought of being drafted; some even dropped out of school and enlisted. Others stayed in school but had dreams of using the high-tech gadgetry used by soldiers: night-vision goggles, powerful guns, and sophisticated computers and lasers that marked kill-sites. A handful of us faced our worst nightmare—the possibility that we would be forced into the Army and have to kill or be killed, or refuse to be drafted and be sent to prison. All of this because we were doing what seemed plain in the Bible!

There never was a draft, but looking back I realize that my decision forced me to claim my convictions as a Christian. During that time I read the Bible and prayed with more intensity than usual. It was then that the words of Jesus leapt off the page and became more real. The courage and strength of those Brethren believers who had walked the path of Christianity before me also became an inspiration. They were men and women who had done the right thing, regardless of the effect it would have on them personally. Throughout Brethren history normal men just like me refused to enter the military not because they were cowards, but because they were compelled by faith—a faith that is timeless, a faith that finds courage in things the world often does not, a faith seeking the kingdom of God.

Today, the decision to be a Christian peacemaker and disciple of Christ may be as hard as ever. But the path we walk as Christian peacemakers is not a solitary one. Many have walked before us and worn this path well, showing us the way. The world around us offers a road that may seem easier to follow—an eight-lane superhighway with more travelers, yet perhaps more potholes. And still new trails will be blazed by Christian peacemakers, people just like you who see a hurting world, but also a world that is full of potential.

The paths lie before us all. Which will you choose?

God's love and peace,
Greg Davidson Laszakovits

Greg Davidson Laszakovits is coordinator of the Church of the Brethren Washington Office.

LETTER TWENTY-SIX
Art Gish

Simpson
W. Institute Place
City, Kansas 53711

Dear youth,

It was a cold evening in Hebron as I sat shivering on the sidewalk. Ziad, an eighteen-year-old Palestinian youth, had been sitting there for three or four hours. After a difficult confrontation with the Israeli soldier who was detaining Ziad, I decided to take off my hat, coat, sweater, and shirt, and suffer with Ziad until the Israeli soldier agreed to release him.

I was engaging in a bit of nonviolent peacemaking as part of Christian Peacemaker Teams, the kind of action I take part in almost every day when in Hebron. But how did I get from being a rebellious Pennsylvania Brethren teenager, ready to go into the military, to a Christian peacemaker engaging in nonviolent action in Palestine?

When I was sixteen, I was planning to go into the military. Though raised in the Church of the Brethren, my high school classmates and teachers had convinced me that war was necessary and good, the best way of solving many human problems. I wanted to be a good American.

But after much soul-searching, I decided at age eighteen to give my whole life to following Jesus. I understood that meant following a different path than what the world offers. What a difference that has made in my life. Although it has been difficult at times, I have never regretted my decision.

After this momentous decision, I entered Brethren Volunteer Service in 1958 and served in Germany and Austria; I worked in the civil rights movement in the 1960s and was part of the Vietnam War protests. Since then I have protested all of America's wars in addition to working for a more loving way of relating to God's creation.

I have become convinced of the utter futility of war and violence. I know of no social, economic, spiritual, or political problem that has been solved by war. After all those lives are wasted and resources destroyed by war, what is left but to pick up the pieces and start over? Think of all the suffering that could be avoided if peace negotiations could happen before instead of at the end of a war.

As I see all this futility, I am repeatedly convinced that Jesus is the way, the truth, and the life. Proud and powerful leaders think they know better than Jesus, but I am certain that it is in Jesus that we see the clearest understanding of truth and reality, that Jesus is the way to salvation.

I am aware of the reality of evil. Horrible things happen in the world. I have seen some of them. I do not believe that evil will go away. There is only one way I know of to overcome evil: the way of nonviolent, suffering love, the way of the cross. God's ultimate way of overcoming evil was to come in Jesus, make himself vulnerable to that evil, take the suffering of evil upon himself, and rise victorious over that evil.

The one way we are commanded to imitate Jesus is to take up the cross, to walk the way of nonviolent love, and to overcome evil with good.

For the past six years, I have been going to Palestine with Christian Peacemaker Teams to be a nonviolent witness in the midst of extreme violence and suffering. I have been privileged to listen to people from all sides, to hear their fears and pain. In the process I have been cursed, spat upon, punched, kicked, and stoned. I have sat in houses that were being stoned and threatened. I have listened to gunfire around me. I have sat with families whose homes were demolished by military bulldozers, agonized with people whose land has been confiscated.

I wish we had thousands of people trained in nonviolence, ready to go into places of conflict to represent God's love in the middle of those conflicts. Instead of soldiers trained to kill, I wish we would send people wanting to heal. I know it is possible. I have seen nonviolence in practice.

I also wish I were young again, with a whole life to be lived for God's glory and my neighbor's good. I wish I still had the energy and enthusiasm of youth. Actually, I still have the enthusiasm but not as much energy.

I have learned that life is very short, too short to be wasted. I have learned that the most exciting, the most fulfilling things I have ever done, were in response to God's call for my life.

I want to encourage you to open your heart to God's love, to tell God you will go wherever God leads you. I dare you to reject hate, fear, and domination and choose a life of openness, love, and service. May you be fulfilled with God's love and peace and be empowered by God's Spirit.

God's peace be with you,
Art Gish

Art Gish is an organic farmer and a Christian Peacemaker Team reservist.

LETTER TWENTY-SEVEN
Yvonne Dilling

Yvonne Dilling, trained in Spanish and peacemaking, set out to test her academic skills in a real life situation and see what it was like to be on the receiving end of US foreign policy. For eighteen months in 1981–82, she worked with aid organizations serving Salvadoran war refugees in Honduras. Her book In Search of Refuge *is her diary of those days and includes this story of a fateful afternoon when she helped ferry dozens of Salvadoran children across the swollen Lempa River while the military showered the area with gunfire.*

We kept bandaging minor wounds until 3:00 p.m., when all of a sudden the flow of refugees stopped. I asked those who were still resting under the tree whether more people would be coming, and they answered, "Oh, there are hundreds! Hundreds and hundreds!" But they weren't arriving. I could not figure out what was keeping them. Finally I asked, "If you say there are hundreds, what is taking them so long to get up here?" A man responded, "Well, they need to cross a deep river, and the few swimmers who can carry them across are exhausted. They, too, have been without food for three days and have been bringing people across on their backs or on makeshift rafts since the early dawn hours. Now they must be resting or going more slowly."

Only then did I truly realize that their flight to Honduras had involved swimming the Lempa River. I questioned further and was shocked to learn that only five men down there knew how to swim. Immediately I decided to go down. We were just sitting here waiting, watching helicopters fly around, and listening to bombs fall. I could not bear the frustration of knowing the imminent danger for all these people while we were doing nothing.

Francesca said she could not go since she did not want to jeopardize the organization for which she worked. I felt glad not to have a commitment to anybody which would keep me from going. Quickly I scratched a message for the Caritas team on a little sheet of paper: "If something happens to me, know that I made the decision I *had* to make," and stuck it in the bottom of Francesca's backpack.

I was fully aware of the danger of walking into a war, but I knew I had no choice. So I informed the Salvadoran who had put himself in charge of keeping the refugees moving that I would help swim people across if someone could guide me down to the river. He burst into tears. "Please," he said, "my three children have not come over, and I have been waiting all day long. Could you please bring them?" He gave me their names, begging me to help. We both cried. I tried to reassure him, "Yes, we'll bring all the children. We'll make sure they all get across."

My guide and I climbed down the hill in a dry creek bed, straight down a rocky path which was so steep that it seemed like a dry waterfall. We barely arrived at the shore full of crying babies and half-naked adults when down that same hill came Ramon, Alejandro, and Paolo from the Caritas team. We smiled at each other and headed into the water....

We had been swimming for not more than thirty minutes when we suddenly heard helicopter noise. I was on the Honduran side of the border, getting ready to head back into the river, when everybody started running for shelter under the gigantic rocks which are strewn on the bank....

The helicopter first swooped down low on the Salvadoran side and started machine-gunning the shoreline. Then it went off down the river, gained height, turned around, swooped down, and fired on the Honduran side.... Those ten minutes spent running around that rock seemed endless. I had never been that close to gunfire before. I could not comprehend it....

But all of a sudden, miraculously, the helicopter flew off. Not a single person had been directly hit. Alejandro and I looked at each other, saying, "Let's go." And we headed back to the river, dove in, and swam across. As soon as they saw us, people on the other side came running down. "Me next! Me next!" They were more frantic than ever.

I had made maybe ten trips across when we heard the helicopter return. This time I was caught on the Salvadoran side. At the sound of the dadadada, we all started running again. But this side didn't have nearly as many places in which to hide....

The helicopter made swoop after swoop .... Over and over again he lay a path of machine gun fire only a foot away from the people in the water. Once he swooped so low that he almost touched the tree tops above us....

Suddenly a bomb exploded within six yards of us. No one was hit but the air blast covered us with dirt, flying debris, leaves, twigs, and stones. Ramon next to me said, "She is bleeding. I think she must have been killed." He was referring to an older woman on the other side of him who was holding a baby—probably her grandchild. A few minutes later he reached over to take the baby. The woman was dead.

Certainly the soldier must have seen that he was firing at women and babies. Some children panicked and ran, but as soon as they did, the helicopter spotted them and turned for another round....

When the helicopter finally left, I felt numb. I had seen only two people killed. How, oh Lord, so few? We could have all been dead. Now, as the terror of the bombardment subsided, I felt the exhaustion from the previous hour of swimming. Padre Ramon said, "We need to go. We'd better get out of here." I was so glad he said it; I could not have taken it any longer, I was so scared.

Reprinted from In Search of Refuge, *by Yvonne Dilling, Herald Press (1984). Used by permission.*

LETTER TWENTY-EIGHT
SueZann Bosler

Dear future Christian leaders,

On September 11, 2001, I saw on TV with my own eyes the second plane flying into the World Trade Center. I was so shocked that I cried and wondered if it was really happening. A sense of pain for the thousands of victims came over me, and I began praying for the millions of people affected by this horrendous event, including the families of the terrorists.

I compared it to my own experience on December 22, 1986, when I saw my father, the Reverend Billy Bosler, stabbed to death. Then I was stabbed and left for dead. I worked 10 ½ years, to spare the life of the perpetrator, James Bernard Campbell, and was finally able to achieve my goal. He received life not death. Let me tell you, I was not able to truly forgive this man until the moment that I finally let go of the anger and bitterness that I felt for him and got on with my life. I had to bring out the good in this situation and let go of the bad. I had come to realize that my hate was not hurting him; it was consuming and hurting me. I remember vividly that Jesus said, "Turn the other cheek," and that is what I did.

I was against the death penalty before these things happened, and now I am striving more adamantly for the end of executions, torture, racism, injustice, and wars of hatred and revenge, so the places that Jesus walked can be restored, and we can all work together to find peace.

What would you do if you were asked to protest war? Well, I know what Mother Teresa would do. She was asked one day if she would join a march against the war, and she replied, "No, but I will be there to walk with you for peace."

So sisters and brothers, I am going to ask you to play a part in this work for peace and justice by making a pledge, which you will find on the Brethren website (brethren.org/genbd/witness/peace/pledge.htm). It states: *I won't fight to kill. I will fight injustice. I will fight hatred. I will fight racism. I will work to make sure that everyone has what they need to live as God intends. I just won't fight to kill.*

I have seen many bumper stickers since 9/11 with flags on them and various patriotic sayings, but if I had a bumper sticker, mine would say, "I am proud to be an American against War, Executions, and Racism" or "United We Stand—for Peace." I hope you will join me in the positive quest for peace and justice, striving to do what Jesus would do.

Paz (peace) and love,
SueZann Bosler

SueZann Bosler is a hair stylist, a victim of violent crime, and an activist against the death penalty.

LETTER TWENTY-NINE
Chuck Boyer

Dear friends,

In 1950–1951, a German exchange student named Siegfried Huebener lived in our family. I was an eighth grader that year and we lived on a small farm in Indiana. Siegfried happily participated in the youth fellowship of our Church of the Brethren. He sometimes spoke of the similarities and differences between our congregation and his Lutheran church back home.

As Christmas approached Siegfried asked my parents if they would be willing to attend the Christmas Eve service at a nearby Lutheran church. Our congregation did not have services on Christmas Eve, and my parents were happy to oblige. On December 24 we found ourselves inside a beautifully decorated sanctuary with banners, candles, and poinsettias adding splendor to the service. I do not remember what was said or done in the service, but I remember the beauty of the sanctuary.

Following worship my mother fixed hot chocolate and we sat around our kitchen table. Siegfried was very pensive and I remember thinking that he must be homesick. Finally Siegfried spoke, "Do you know what I have been thinking? I was thinking that six years ago the people we were worshiping with tonight were praying that the American bombers would fly straight and the American gunners would shoot straight so that they would kill the people worshiping tonight in my home church in Schluechtern. And six years ago the people worshiping in my church in Germany were praying that the German bombers would fly straight and the German gunners would shoot straight so that they would kill the people with whom we just worshiped. And it doesn't make any sense. It doesn't make any sense!"

Some years later, in the summer of 1958, I appeared before my local draft board to ask to be classified as a conscientious objector to war. Although I never liked to fight and was opposed to violent solutions to problems, I recognized that there was a violent streak within me. I became furious with people I saw taking advantage of the weak and defenseless. The task of draft boards at that time was to determine whether someone was sincerely opposed to all wars, so I knew they would ask difficult questions. In the course of my interview, one of the men told me of his son who had been killed fourteen years earlier in the war against Japan. The story, I felt, was meant to say to me, "My son loved his country and gave his life for it. You are a coward and don't deserve to live here." As the man went on, he became more and more emotional, and at the end of the story he broke down and cried. All I could say was, "I'm sure you loved your son and he did what he thought was right. I cannot and will not train to kill other people." I did not say that I was totally nonviolent and never became angry. But I had come to know that I could not train to use weapons of violence.

In 1959–1960, I served in Brethren Volunteer Service in Germany. Because I had experience with an exchange student brother from that country, I was very interested in learning how the Germans had allowed their nation to succumb to Nazism. As I learned to know German Christians, I would ask them how they explained the events that led up to the Second World War. Almost always I received two responses. First, I was told that when people began to hear of the Nazi atrocities they could not believe that their nation would allow such things to happen. And if they did finally accept the possibility that concentration camps and mass murder of Jews were real, it was too dangerous for people to speak out. That I could understand and I knew what courage it took to resist their evil government.

The second response has troubled me much more. Many of the Christians I spoke with claimed that because the scriptures say that all government is "ordained" by God, the Creator must have wanted the Nazis to come to power. Their response was, "We don't know why God would have wanted it to happen, but it must have been his will." I have never accepted this way of thinking. We have governments because we need ways to regulate groups of people. Some governments are concerned with God's will and some are not. The Christian is called to disobey governments and laws that forbid worship, promote evil, or destroy human life.

One of the questions often asked of people who refuse to support violence is, "What would happen if everyone believed the way you do?" My response is, "Wouldn't it be wonderful to have a world where everyone believed in settling conflicts without fighting?" But it does not appear that a majority of the world's citizens will espouse nonviolence in the near future.

Our Christian faith can give us the courage to live nonviolently even when we're a minority, because we believe that there is eternal life. With all the mistakes we make, we believe that if we follow the teachings of Jesus, nothing can separate us from God's love. If I die in an automobile accident, I will not be separated from God's love. If I die from cancer, I will not be separated from God's love. If I am killed by violent people, I will not be separated from God's love. And I know that I am going to die sometime. Therefore, I do not have to destroy other lives to try to protect my own, which will end someday.

Peace,
Chuck Boyer

Chuck Boyer is a retired pastor from La Verne, California, former peace consultant for the General Board, and Annual Conference moderator in 1993.

LETTER THIRTY
Robert Miller

Dear fellow Christians,

"Continuing the Work of Jesus. Peacefully. Simply. Together." It looks good on paper. It even sounds good from the pulpit, but what does it really mean to continue the work of Jesus *peacefully*? Does it mean not resisting evildoers and turning the other cheek (Matt. 5:39), even when it's ridiculed as weakness? Does it mean loving the enemy and praying for those who persecute us (Matt. 5:44) when it's perceived as unpatriotic? Does it mean putting our sword back into its place (Matt. 26:52) when it's laughed at as idealistic? Does it mean taking up a cross and following Jesus (Mark 8:34) instead of taking up a gun and following the crowd? Does it mean actually doing what Jesus did and what he commanded us to do as well?

This seems to me a fundamental question, because it asks if being Christian requires us to take seriously the example and teachings of Jesus. It's puzzling to me that most Christians I know quote the Old Testament more than they quote Jesus when it comes to capital punishment and war. And it's perplexing to me that the historic peace churches—Brethren, Mennonites, and Quakers—are regarded by many Christians as naive, if not foolish, for rejecting violence and retaliation, even though Jesus did.

The bottom line for me is what we, as Christians, pledge our allegiance to. If we pledge allegiance to the powers that be, we will continue the work of war because it's the "sensible" thing to do. But if we pledge allegiance to the kingdom of God, we will continue the work of peace because it's the faithful thing to do, no matter how idealistic, impractical, or unpatriotic it may seem. After all, if God is for this way of being in the world, who can ultimately be against it?

May God give you courage, strength, and joy to continue the work of Jesus peacefully in this world.
Robbie Miller

Robert R. Miller is campus pastor at Bridgewater College in Virginia.

LETTER THIRTY-ONE
Dale Aukerman

Dale Aukerman patterned his life after Jesus. He lived simply in an eigh-teenth-century log cabin near New Windsor, Maryland. He kept his income low by volunteering and preaching the gospel part time. And he worked tirelessly protesting the stockpiling of nuclear missiles, visiting death row inmates, and writing books with a powerful message of peace. Dale died of cancer in the fall of 1999. These excerpts from Paul Grout's comments at Dale's funeral service are a window into a peace-maker's soul.

Some time ago, fairly early on in the battle [against cancer], while I was visiting Dale, he took me aside and said: "Paul, Ruth and I would like you to preach at my memorial service. We want this because we know that we can trust you to lift up Jesus Christ and not Dale Aukerman."

By now as I stand before you I have a problem. I understood what Dale was saying and I agree. It's just that I'm not so very sure of what was Dale and what was Jesus. Was it Dale who visited Ronnie Dunkins on death row, or was it Christ? Was it Dale who witnessed the execution or Christ? Was it Dale who wept, or was it Christ?

Jesus Christ protested against a country that had lost its way.

Jesus Christ was arrested in Washington.

Was I standing next to Dale, or was I standing with Christ at the barbed wire fence between us and the armed soldiers guarding horrible weapons of unimaginable destructive power?

Did Dale's truth-telling keep him from rising in our denomination, or was Christ kept from rising?

Sitting at the Aukerman table, I recognized Christ in the breaking of the bread.

Christ comes to us through the Holy Spirit, he comes to us through the least in society, he comes to us through scripture, and Christ comes to us in one another.

> *From now on, therefore, we regard no one from a human point of view; even though we once knew Christ from a human point of view, we know him no longer in that way. So if anyone is in Christ, there is a new creation; everything old has passed away; see, every-thing has become new! (2 Cor. 5:16-17).*

And it is no longer I who live, but it is Christ who lives in me. And the life I now live in the flesh I live by faith in the Son of God, who loved me and gave himself for me (Gal. 2:20).

Now by this we may be sure that we know him, if we obey his commandments. Whoever says, "I have come to know him," but does not obey his commandments, is a liar, and in such a person, the truth does not exist; but whoever obeys his word, truly in this person the love of God has reached perfection. By this we may be sure that we are in him; whoever says, "I abide in him," ought to walk just as he walked (1 John 2:3-6).

In giving ourselves over to Christ, the Holy Spirit dwells within us. His life resounds within us. We pattern our lives either after Jesus Christ or after someone or something else. Even our language, our particular dialect, betrays our unconscious patterning. Social scientists can usually tell which area of the country we grew up in by listening to us speak. Our attitude, thought process, and action are more dictated by the world than we often realize.

A friend told a story of an incident that occurred in his hometown. A man had an accident that permanently damaged one of his legs. For the rest of his life he would walk with a noticeable limp. The man married and this union produced a healthy baby boy. The child grew up in the small town among family, friends, neighbors, and a close knit church community. No one noticed anything wrong until the boy went to school. His kindergarten teacher was from another town and had never seen the boy before his first day of school. At the end of that day, the teacher went to the school nurse and asked what had happened to the child, causing him to walk with a limp. Of course, the boy so admired and loved his father that he wanted to be just like him in every way.

Our lives will be patterned; intentionally or unintentionally they will be patterned. Dale Aukerman sought to pattern his life after Jesus. We saw this in the way he walked.

....Dale Aukerman was not a great man. Do not diminish his life by designating him so. Dale Aukerman was not a good man. He would never claim for himself a designation that Christ rejected for himself. If Dale was great and good, he was an exception, and we don't have to deal personally with his life. This is what we saw: we saw the One in Dale to whom he gave his life. To be sure, we saw Dale, a unique person, unique to all others on earth, but we saw this too: a human being, a soul alive, made alive in Christ.

Reprinted from Hope Beyond Healing, *Brethren Press, 2000.*

LETTER THIRTY-TWO
Celia Cook-Huffman

Dear youth,

I grew up in a Brethren world. My parents were children of people who were involved in the church, and their parents' parents had been involved in the church—the legacy is long. I can't remember when I realized that this "story" had created a path for my life, but I can articulate pieces of the story that define that path. There are two I would like to share about my grandparents.

On my father's side of the family was my Grandpa Cook. He was a conscientious objector in WWI. What I know from studying nonviolence is that this was a very tough time to be a pacifist. The men were scattered and isolated from one another. The alternative service options that existed in WWII didn't exist during WWI. What I know from family stories is that for my grandfather this meant he had to serve as a cook in an Army unit, but refused to carry a gun. For this stance he was tarred and feathered. I don't remember my grandfather ever talking about this event, but I knew it happened. As a child I remember trying to imagine what it must have felt like. What did it mean to have to live in that place? Did he have any friends? How did he get through it? There were other scattered stories about him. One involved him facing down the Ku Klux Klan. The details are all vague, but the message I took away was clear. Being Brethren meant being different; it meant doing things that were hard and scary because they were the right things to do, and it meant sticking up for people who couldn't always stick up for themselves.

On my mother's side of the family were Grandma and Grandpa Snider. They were farmers in Ohio. We went to visit them a couple of times each year. They were generous people. As a child I remember them taking in "strays"—nephews who needed a place to go, cousins looking for work. The stories about my grandparents and the farm were stories of generosity and welcome. The sense I have of this hospitality was that it was "normal." They weren't looking for guests. In many cases they weren't looking for help on the farm. On the other hand, they didn't resent the extra bodies, or the extra mouths to feed. It was what you did. People needed help, people needed a place to go, you offered whatever you could. There was no arrogance to their giving; they were not better than those they helped. Nor was there any particular humility. It was just what you did.

This expectation of taking care of others also became fundamental to my sense of what it means to be Brethren. My Uncle Max went with Heifer Project to Germany to take care of others. My mother was in Brethren Volunteer Service (BVS) after WWII, taking care of others. What was important was that you gave with grace. You did not pass judgment in your giving, or give to change the other person. You took care of those in need; you shared what you had to share.

I went to Manchester College to be a physical therapist. By the end of my freshman year I had migrated to peace studies. There were probably a lot of reasons for this choice. But among them, central in ways I didn't understand at the time, was the rightness of the path. Here was a place I could live my values in my work. That was what I had learned from my grandparents. Believing in a set of rules or in a right way to live comes *alive* when you live it.

All around me as a child I saw people living their beliefs, making choices, hard choices because of their beliefs. Being Brethren does not mean I am going to have a comfortable life. Instead, it means I have to be willing to take risks and do scary things. It means being willing to stand up for myself and for what I believe in, and to stand up and speak when others are being silenced. It means taking care of others and sharing what I have with grace. The legacy of my grandparents is to live your values. Peace studies have given me a place to live that legacy, to honor my heritage, and I hope to model it for those in the next generation.

Peace,
Celia Cook-Huffman

Celia Cook-Huffman is assistant professor of peace studies and associate director of the Baker Institute for Peace and Conflict Studies at Juniata College.

LETTER THIRTY-THREE
Phil Rieman

Dear youth,

I turned eighteen in August of 1962 during the very early stages of the Vietnam War. Growing up in a Church of the Brethren home that was steeped in concern for peace and justice, I was given the clear teaching that "all war is sin" and contrary to the will of God and that all human life is precious. So it was natural that as a follower of Christ I would embrace pacifism.

At the time I was of draft age, the Selective Service System was conscripting soldiers for service, but the system was set up to recognize conscientious objector (CO) status, so one could register for the draft and then immediately apply for CO status. Objectors, of course, had to prove to the draft board that their beliefs were deeply held and that they were opposed to all war, not just certain wars. But that wasn't too difficult in Wabash County where there were a fair number of members of the Church of the Brethren and the Society of Friends (Quakers).

I remember seriously considering non-registration, because I believed that the Selective Service System was really a system of death, in essence, designed to induct as many young men as possible for the express purpose of killing in time of war. But because there was a system in place that allowed objectors to do alternative service in lieu of military service, and because my parents and church saw alternative service as more "constructive" and "practical" than being imprisoned for refusing to register, I chose alternative service. I was glad to be able to work and learn through Brethren Volunteer Service in the inner city of Baltimore. It was a great experience.

Yet as I reflect on that period of my life, I feel that I didn't listen carefully enough to the "still small voice" of God within me, which I think was calling me more strongly toward resistance (the non-registration position) than I gave credit at the time. I suspect that has a lot to do with my subsequent leanings about war and the decision my wife and I made when we first earned a taxable income. We decided that if bodily participation in war was morally wrong for us, then paying someone else to kill in our names through a system of federal taxation was also wrong for us. Modern war has come to rely more on high-tech weaponry and material and depend less on "warm bodies" to do the killing, thus decreasing the need for conscription of young recruits and depending more on the uninterrupted conscription of taxes for war-making.

So I challenge you today with this question: If you pray for peace, how can you pay for war? As you seek ways to say NO to the war machine in this country (through non-participation in the military, or non-registration for the draft, or non-payment of war taxes, or letters of protest to Congress or the local newspaper editor, or living more simply, i.e., below a taxable income), may you be equally fervent in saying YES to life! You can do this by serving others in need, locally or far away; giving generously to the church and other charities; actively promoting restorative justice; or doing whatever you can to remove the systemic causes of war and building, instead, a culture of peace in its place!

In doing these things, may you join other like-minded people to enlarge and flesh out your vision for a better world, at the same time being sure to balance your need for both action and reflection—in a way that keeps you healthy in your relationships with others and growing and whole as a child and servant of God.

Blessings for the journey!

Peace,
Phil Rieman

Phil Rieman is co-pastor of the Northview Church of the Brethren in Indianapolis, Indiana, and with his wife, Louise, a military tax resister.

LETTER THIRTY-FOUR
Chandler Edwards

Brethren Volunteer Service worker Chandler Edwards was killed while doing rural development work in Laos during the Vietnam War.... He died April 24, 1969. The US government report said he was killed while returning from a trip to a village school-building project. His jeep was hit by a rocket, and two of his passengers also died. Other passengers said the ambush was by the North Vietnamese-aligned Pathet Lao and that Chandler had earlier contacted Lao Army authorities who said the road was secure. Chandler had worked two years in Laos and was close to completing his term.... He planned to return to Laos after a visit in the US. The following is from a letter he wrote to BVS staff.

Just sitting here singing by myself without another person around close by and I got to feeling so good all over. I just couldn't keep it inside me anymore.... Do you recall how we (used) to sit around and talk at all hours of the night, sometimes permitting our temperature to rise, other times everyone was in one accord; the times we used to listen as someone played the guitar and sang and the sound thereof taking one off into the remotest recesses of the mind....

Now, in this day of modern warfare when a person can aim an object at others and the others become covered completely with burning sensations, yes, even burns, what does this do to the morals of the person doing this tragic thing? Have the American people ... become so insensitive that (they) will permit such outrage against mankind to continue?

It moves me from the very depths of my being to see this happening and yet, just what the blazes can we do? As a result of the war in Vietnam, the forgotten war in Laos is permitting American taxpayers' dollars to do this thing also in Laos ... but on an extremely hush hush basis.

News of what is happening in Laos is of the most censored kind I am sure.... Daily I can see American planes loaded to the flying limit with death-delivering explosives go across my head and deliver their arsenal upon the citizens of Laos, many who are loyal to the Lao government and not in sympathy to the cause of Communist Pathet Lao ....

Dead people, blood, a man with his guts in his hands, a woman with a dead two-month-old child in her arms slowly rocking back and forth in the ruins of her destroyed house, a small lad blinded by napalm, driven mentally off balance and crying for mother who is dead and only several yards from him but he can't see her.

I tell you it is enough to drive a person crazy to have this go on in the area where you live and are trying to establish some kind of community development programs only to see it (destroyed) slowly at times and swiftly at others by the uncaring Americans in the sky who release this deadly hell from the belly of their planes not knowing any of the people it kills or forever cripples, leaves sightless, etc. etc. I get so discouraged I could walk in the jungle and never return.

The directions from the American Embassy come to be more and more guarded in what we write to anyone in the States, but I'm past caring anymore. I was talking to a CIA agent in Vientiane last week when I had to go there for medical treatment and he was telling me that in his personal opinion, the censored, forgotten, and bedamned war in Laos will become larger, more destructive, more censored, etc. before it lets up.

I've written some very direct and nasty letters to people in the States in addition to talking with the North Vietnamese Embassy in Laos, the Red Chinese Embassy, the Russian Embassy, Indian, Cambodia, French, English, and the Pathet Lao headquarters upon various points of mutual interest at this time, and am under threat of being forced to leave the country by USAID and the beloved American Embassy for my actions.

I may be called a communist and a traitor but I'll stand by what I believe in until the day I draw my last breath. The American Embassy here and the ambassador himself called me on the carpet. They have the policy that an American in Laos is to have no kind of contact in any way, shape, or fashion with the enemy. Since I did, my head (is) due to roll.

In a long conference with the ambassador in which he called me a traitor or a communist, he said he was going to start proceedings to have my visa revoked and to have me thrown physically, legally, and bodily from the country. As a result I offered the threat of blowing higher than hell stories to magazines, newspapers—straight, liberal, conservative, and radical right and left . . . .

I see a wide-open road in the future with unlimited opportunity to work with people for people, helping anyone in any way except with (violence). Since I've come to Laos I've become more and more of a radical, still a solid pacifist, more concerned with the needs of others and think less and less of self-gain, more convinced that the American government is going down (the) road of self-destruction. Only regret more don't raise voices of protest.

Reprinted from Messenger *(January 1992). Used by permission.*

LETTER THIRTY-FIVE
Shawn Flory Replogle

Nicholas Jones
255 Maple Drive
Cottage, Tennessee 97314

Dear friends,

Jesus says, "You have heard that it was said, 'You shall love your neighbor and hate your enemy.' But I say to you, Love your enemies and pray for those who persecute you, so that you may be children of your Father in heaven; for he makes his sun rise on the evil and on the good, and sends rain on the righteous and on the unrighteous. For if you love those who love you, what reward have you? Do not even the tax collectors do the same? And if you greet only your brothers and sisters, what more are you doing than others? Do not even the Gentiles do the same? Be perfect, therefore, as your heavenly Father is perfect'" (Matt. 5:43-48).

What challenging words. But they get right to the heart of the matter. It's easier to love those who love me. I know they will love me back. But to love those who may not like me, or who I think may hate me, well, that's nearly impossible. If I try to love my enemy, I am completely vulnerable, at their mercy. It's so easy for me to dismiss Jesus' words as idealistic, as nice thoughts, but way too lofty and unattainable.

Later on in the Gospel of Matthew, when Jesus is confronted by an angry mob seeking his arrest and demise, he scolds his followers who draw blood with their sword: "Put your sword back into its place; for all who take the sword will perish by the sword. Do you think that I cannot appeal to my Father, and he will at once send me more than twelve legions of angels? But how then would the scriptures be fulfilled, which say it must happen in this way!" (Matt. 26:52-54).

We know that Jesus actually could have called on legions of angels. In Jesus' temptation in the desert, even Satan knew that Jesus had that kind of authority. But Jesus resisted the easy way out, the short cut, the testing of God's power: "Do not put the Lord your God to the test" (Matt. 4:7).

So Jesus talked a good talk: Love your enemies; put away your sword. But did he ever put his money where his mouth is, so to speak?

Does a cross come to mind?

At the hands of the religious authorities, Jesus was humiliated, beaten, whipped, spat on, and finally nailed to two wooden beams. In that moment, Jesus was as vulnerable as a Palestinian baby born to a teenage mother and a carpenter. A common thief heckled him: "Are you not the Messiah? Save yourself and us!" (Luke 23:39). All the while, Jesus displayed love for them: "Father, forgive them; for they do not know what they are doing" (Luke 23:34).

At the same time, on the cross, Jesus had all the power of heaven and earth at his disposal. Jesus could have called on God's angels to release him; he could have unleashed the mightiest, most destructive war this world has ever seen, all to have himself taken down from the suffering of the cross. Jesus, in that moment, was all-powerful. What he chose in that moment would and should instruct us for all of eternity.

Jesus did nothing and yet he did everything. As he had in life, Jesus shamed those allied against him. He revealed the wickedness of the world by letting the world do what it does best—simply be its violent self. Jesus portrayed the single greatest moment of nonviolent resistance we will ever witness. And what was his reward? He was exalted to the right hand of God.

While being exalted to God's right hand is remarkable in itself, I find it more remarkable in light of the fact that for three years Jesus taught that to be exalted you must humble yourself (Matt. 23:12). He, the King of kings, washed his disciples' feet (John 13). Jesus taught that to save your life, you must lose it, (Matt. 16:24-26), and lose it he did on the cross, which makes Jesus all the more remarkable. Jesus was wholly consistent. He practiced what he preached.

We've lost sight of how hard it is to be consistent in our world. Think of the political rhetoric around such issues as abortion and the death penalty. How many politicians have you heard who have proclaimed themselves to be "pro life" and at the same time for the death penalty. Wouldn't someone with a true pro-life stance object to killing a human who has killed a human to show that killing humans is wrong?

Which only shows how tough consistency really is. And which shows how amazing Jesus was. He must have been of God, a full revelation of God, which is why I follow him—to be saved from the inconsistencies of my own living. And if I follow, I am bound to aspire to the same consistency, humbling myself, choosing nonviolent ways, shaming those who seek my own (physical, spiritual, emotional) death. This is why I choose the way of nonviolence, simple living, relationship building, and reconciliation with God—because Jesus demands consistency from me.

Children and youth look to adults as role models, listening to what they say and watching what they do. Children look for consistency. As a Christian, I look to Jesus in the same way. I look to "Jesus the pioneer and perfecter of our faith, who for the sake of the joy that was set before him endured the cross, disregarding its shame, and has taken his seat at the right hand of the throne of God" (Heb. 12:2). I know that Jesus would not sit in a fighter plane and drop bombs because that is not consistent with the cross. Are my actions consistent with the cross? Are my actions consistent with Jesus Christ, the Son of God? Jesus' words weren't expressed merely to be appreciated. They were expressed to be lived, lived out in a consistent faith in Jesus, our Lord and Savior.

In Jesus' name,
Shawn Flory Replogle

Shawn Flory Replogle is pastor of the South Waterloo Church of the Brethren and a past coordinator of National Youth Conference.

LETTER THIRTY-SIX
Dale Brown

Dear sisters and brothers,

Do not dismiss the gospel of peace until you have considered and discussed it with those who followed a different drummer than one from our militant culture. Without a draft law, we can't rule out the possibility of conscription of both men and women. Now is the time to begin to think through how you might respond and what you believe.

The Brethren stance emerges in times of violence, war, and hatred. Our witness is needed. The gospel of peace is both liberal and conservative. It is liberal in that it embraces deep concerns for compassion, justice, and reconciliation of relationships, both personal and between nations. It is conservative in that it invites us to follow Jesus. Brethren take Jesus seriously. Jesus says if you love him you will keep his commandments. And two of his commands are to love our enemies and pray for those who persecute us. Jesus blessed peacemakers, not war-makers, as children of God.

Many protest that our position is passive, that we are willing to be doormats and let others walk over us. But many of us have experienced peacemaking to be more than that. It is not passive but active. it is not defeating, but deeply satisfying. For instance, many Brethren in Europe participated in memorable ways with the American army and the Marshall Plan in the rehabilitation of Europe. It was wonderful to make friends of former enemies of our nation. Then, in the long war in Vietnam, many Brethren who are church leaders today, served in a variety of ways rather than fighting a war that was proven to be immoral, mistaken, and impossible to win apart from using nuclear weapons. More recently Brethren and Mennonites responded to the call of the Red Cross and the Salvation Army to come to New York to minister to the grieving and to care for children from families who were victims of the tragic acts of the terrorists.

In addition to being faithful and satisfying, the peace position actually works. My grandfather told me stories of an earlier time about bandits riding horses to rob his little grocery store on the plains of Kansas. He related how other merchants got killed because they attempted to shoot it out with the robbers, while Brethren, though losing some money, were not harmed because Brethren did not have guns. Though it is true that people who do not have guns are often killed, his explanation has a measure of truth. The twentieth century, with two big wars and many smaller wars, experienced successful nonviolent movements. Through nonviolent resistance Gandhi gained freedom from India; Martin Luther

King, Jr., led the nonviolent movement to gain rights for Blacks; non-cooperation of teachers in Norway maintained freedom against Hitler; the people of Iran gained freedom from the brutal Shah; many Eastern European nations gained independence from puppet rulers of the Soviet Union. These stories all demonstrate victories achieved through nonviolent resistance of unarmed people over heavily armed adversaries without the bloodshed and hatred that result from rebellions and wars.

The way of peace is not just a thing of the past. In fact, our heritage of peace makes more sense today than any time I can remember. Pacifists today are advocating that our nation give birth to the unexpected, for this "war against terrorism" is a different kind of war. We need to understand the root of the anger of those called terrorists. We need to launch programs that will eliminate the soil where terror germinates. The cycle of violence must be penetrated with the good news of peace.

If violence were the way to deal with terrorism, Israel would be the safest place to be in the world. Jesus' teaching to abandon an eye-for-an-eye and a tooth-for-a-tooth strategy has been vindicated many times and led Gandhi to quip that retaliation will leave the whole world blind and tooth-less if continued. American bombings with superior weapons will only create more terrorists. The answer is not in becoming like the terrorists, but in making friends. As the New Testament teaches us, there is not fear in love. For Christians, love casts out fear. We have our security in Jesus, not in the power of our nation.

The solution will be in acts of redemptive love, not in more and more armaments that will sap the strength of America. It is because we love our nation that we cannot cooperate with militaristic strategies of violence that have led all nations seeking world domination to end up on the ash heap of history.

Join Jesus (not the armed forces) who wept over Jerusalem when the zealots were planning rebellion against Roman rule. Jesus cried out: "Oh that they would know the things that make for peace."

Peace,
Dale Brown

Dale W. Brown is a retired professor from Bethany Theological Seminary and former director of the seminary's peace studies program.

~

Epitaph

We exhort the brethren to steadfastness in the faith, and believe that the times in which our lots are cast strongly demand of us a strict adherence to all our principles, and especially to our non-resistant principle, a principle dear to every subject of the Prince of Peace, and a prominent doctrine of our Fraternity, and to endure whatever sufferings and to make whatever sacrifice the maintaining of the principle may require, and not to encourage in any way the practice of war ....

Annual Meeting minutes, 1864